Economic and Ecological Dimensions of Livestock Economy

Economic and Ecological Dimensions of Livestock Economy

An Indian Case Study of Small Ruminants

Syed Ajmal Pasha

Commonwealth

Economic and Ecological Dimensions of Livestock Economy

Ist Edition : 2001
ISBN 81-7169-654-6

Published by :
Ajay Verma
For Commonwealth Publishers
4831/24, Prahlad Street,
Ansari Road, Darya Ganj,
New Delhi - 110002
Phone : 3272541, 3257835
Fax: 91-011-3257835

Laser Typesetting by:
Stylish Laser Typesetter
Delhi

Printed at:
Efficient Offset Printers
Shahzada Bagh, Delhi

Dedicated
to
My Parents and
Prof. M.V. Nadkarni

FOREWORD

The livestock economy in India has registered an impressive growth since 1970. The share of this sector in GDP has increased threefold, *i.e.* from 2.8 percent in 1970-71 to about 9 percent in 1996-97. What is even more important, the sector has contributed to sustaining and improving the livelihoods of millions people, especially of those engaged in marginal agriculture in drought-prone parts of the arid and semi-arid zones of the country.

Within the livestock sector, the small ruminants covering goats and sheep are particularly important for their contribution to sustaining livelihoods in terms of income and employment generation and in sheltering risk and uncertainty of poor households. Since small ruminants neither require heavy investment nor involve costly maintenance, they are easily accessible and hence, have the potential for wider distribution of benefits among poor and vulnerable groups. At the same time, it must be noted that they can have a significant negative ecological impact as they are maintained mostly under open grazing conditions, expecially in the ecologically fragile areas. With the expansion of cultivation area and consequent reduction in the common areas for open grazing, the increase in the population of small ruminants can place a severe pressure on the already fragile areas. Here lies the basic conflict between the economic contributions and ecological implications of small ruminants in particular and livestock sector in general. What is the magnitude of this tradeoff? How can such tradeoffs be mediated and resolved through appropriate economic and institutional means? The present analytical study by Dr. Syed Ajmal Pasha is an effort to provide answers to these and related questions. In this study, the author uses primary information from a carefully conducted household survey in selected regions of Karnataka besides from secondary data related to state and national levels to draw important inferences.

Dr. Pasha pursues an interesting approach of contrasting the economics of small ruminants as perceived at the household level with their ecological impact as evaluated at the regional level. Under profit maximising conditions, the author has estimated the cost and profit functions for various rural socio-economic groups. Based on these estimated functions, the author has identified the economic conditions that characterize the optimal flock/herd size under various conditions. The economic analysis is then supplemented to incorporate the equity element by focussing on inter-class differences in the share both in the number of and benefits from small ruminants. In addition to the intra-generational equity questions, inter-generational equity issues are also analysed in terms of long-term ecological consequences of present economic activities. Dr. Pasha's study provides a good understanding of the inter-relationship between small ruminant production and common property resources from a regional perspective.

Based on his detailed analysis, Dr. Pasha has identified some interesting issues, which have considerable significance both for theory and policy. Although scale economic considerations suggest the optimum herd size to be much larger than that is held by different groups, the declining size and increasing degradations of the common property resources that currently support the small ruminants are now becoming a binding constraint for any further expansion. He has also shown that the social costs of rearing small ruminants can be much different from the private costs, especially when there is a strong dependence on common property resources. As we extend this result, we find that the magnitude to the difference between private and social costs depends directly on the intensity of such dependence on common property resources as well as their present ecological status. As the negative ecological effects emerge more from uncontrolled expansion and inefficient management of common property resources, the solution lies in incorporating social costs while estimating the returns. This calls for participatory and community-based institutional arrangement both for regulating the herd size and its distribution as well as for maintaining the ecological health of the resource base.

I congratulate Dr. Pasha for undertaking this important study. This, in my view, is an important contribution to this neglected area of ecological economics. I am sure, this will be an important references work for the students, researchers, non-governmental organizations, and policy-makers with an interest in the interface between ecology, economics, and institutions.

Institute for Social and Economic Change,
Banglore-560072.

M. Govinda Rao
Director

PREFACE

Research on small ruminants (goats and sheep) in India by the social scientists was a neglected subject, even though goats and sheep contribute substantially to the livelihood and farming systems of rural households. Not much work has been done on the socio-economic aspects of small ruminants. The focus, so far has been on agricultural research and development. In animal husbandry too, a lion's share of research and developmental activities has been on large ruminants like cattle and buffalloes.

The present study on the economic, ecological, and equity aspects of small ruminants aims to fill the serious vacuum in the empirical literature on goats and sheep. It grows out of my research work carried out at the Institute for Social and Economic Change (ISEC) since my doctoral work. Several contributed directly or indirectly to the research reported here. This study, in particular, owes much to Prof. M.V. Nadkarni for his constant support and valuable guidance.

I am grateful to Shri T.R. Satish Chandran, Dr. P.V. Shenoi, Prof. S.N. Mishra, Prof. Abdul Aziz, Prof. P.H. Rayappa and Prof. V.M. Rao for their comments and suggestions from time to time. My thanks are also due to Shri M. Vivekananda for his kind help.

The research reported here may not have been seen the light but for the constant encouragement and support of Prof. M. Govinda Rao, our Director, who has also been generous enough in giving an opt foreword. It is also important to thank Prof. R. Maria Saleth for his valuable support, and cooperation. Shri T. Amarnath and S. Padmavathy deserves full appreciation for the excellent secretarial support.

Finally, my thanks are also due to the Commonwealth Publishers for their timely and quality publication of the book.

Syed Ajmal Pasha

PREFACE

CONTENTS

LIST OF TABLES

DIAGRAMS/CHART

1 INTRODUCTION

1.1 Introduction

There are wide differences in India's rural areas in terms of topography, soil, rainfall, water, agro-climatic conditions, agricultural production and productivity. It is useful to broadly classify them into three types of regions-droughtprone, non-droughtprone and mixed. Droughtprone or semi-arid regions pose special problems due to their limited resource endowments like low and uncertain rainfall, low yield in crop production, low fodder base and hence ill-health and lower productivity of livestock and a low diversification of the economy. Strategies for rural development need to be tailored according to the needs of different regions. Irrigation has been a widely accepted strategy to convert droughtprone areas into better endowed ones, but obviously it cannot reach all droughtprone areas or all villages and households in these areas. There is also the strategy of dry land development, but concentrating on crop cultivation alone may not be enough to develop dry areas. That is where the role of animal husbandry becomes relevant particularly in diversifying the rural economy of droughtprone areas and providing additional sources of income. There are of course complementarities between crop cultivation and animal husbandry. While the former provides feed to the latter, the latter provides manure, draught power and additional income through products like milk, meat and wool. The diversification of the rural economy of semi-arid areas, therefore, need not be at the cost of crop husbandry. The complementarities can ensure that both crop and animal husbandry can prosper.

1.2 Significance of Small Ruminants (Sheep and Goats)

Under animal husbandry, a lion's share of development programmes has gone to schemes like 'operation flood' oriented to cows and buffaloes, *i.e.*, to large ruminants. These may not, however, suit droughtprone areas due to limited fodder resources available there. The role of small ruminants in general and in droughtprone areas in particular needs greater attention. Small ruminants have unique qualities of being adaptable to diverse conditions and they have a higher survival rate than cattle or buffaloes. Their small size enables them to survive and flourish on stubbles, herbages and bushes (Winrock, 1983, p. 7).

In droughtprone areas, rearing of small ruminants helps the rural households, especially small and marginal farmers and landless labourers either as main or subsidiary occupation. It helps them to survive better during and after drought. The typical climatic and environmental conditions with low crop yield, more barren lands with very less fodder availability and over grazed pastures/grazing lands by the large ruminants make keeping small ruminants more viable in these regions than large ruminants.

Small ruminants require much less fodder than large ruminants. They can flourish without any concentrated food. Ranjhan assumes 3 tonnes of dry matter per head of large ruminants per year and equates 8 small ruminants to one adult large ruminant in terms of feed intake (Ranjhan, 1986). Askew and Mitchell (1978, as quoted by R. Soedomo and others, 1986) argue that forages from trees and shrubs can contribute only 10 per cent of total diet in cattle in times of drought and this proportion will be much more in the diet of sheep and goats. Moore also is of the opinion that ownership of milch animals is almost entirely confined to those with direct access to some bulk source of fodder (Moore, 1978). On the otherhand, goats can subsist on non-commercial and free sources of fodder of an inferior variety which large ruminants cannot eat. For example, they consume even the tender thorny bushes.

In terms of conversion of fodder into milk, small ruminants are economical than cattle. Goat is even more economical than sheep. Where it is not possible to keep a cow, it is economical to keep a goat for milk. Goat is almost 135 per cent more economical than cattle, since we can get 185 kgs milk per 100 kg digestible organic matter from goats, whereas this figure is 162 kgs milk in the case of cows. Small ruminants need less labour and low cost housing and equipment. It is argued by G. M. M. Lal (1982) that goat milk production is the cheapest.

During and after drought, small ruminants help the farmers as their more dependable assets. They support the farmers, especially those with no other means of income, and also agricultural labourers in terms of milk, wool and by their own liquidity. During droughts, when the small and poor farmers lose their kharif crop, they can depend to some extent on these animals. Farmers are able to sustain their stock of small ruminants even in severe droughts while it is not so in the case of large ruminants. The loss during drought due to distress sale and death of animals is much higher for large ruminants than for small ruminants. Borkar and Nadkarni have pointed out how the cultivator households lose their assets during droughts through distress sale and death of animals due to scarcity of fodder. Among the different types of assets considered, decline (in value terms) was greatest in draught animals followed by cows and buffaloes, but least in other animals, mainly small ruminants (Borkar and Nadkarni, 1975, esp. pp. 28 - 37).

Income from the rearing of small ruminants is also substantially high. Due to easy and cheap management the net income to the farmer is also high. The manure of small ruminants is valuable to the farmer. It is not used as fuel, unlike dung and it is highly nutritious for crop cultivation. Also small ruminants spread the manure and urine very evenly.

As it has been pointed out by Alaev that a Kani of Land (1.32 acres) might be manured well if a flock of 1000 sheep and goats spend five or six nights on it. And after that, the fields produced well for six or seven years (Alaev, 1984).

Some environmentalists have expressed fears over the role of small ruminants in further deteriorating the environment. They (particularly goats) are alleged to prevent regeneration of trees, since they can eat more varieties of plants and can reach where large ruminants cannot. Goats could pose a grave threat to presently emphasised schemes of social forestry and farm forestry. It is however easier to stall-feed both sheep and goats and perhaps economical also (Kalia, 1985). They can be stall-fed through cultivating fodder trees like neem, subabul, khejri, kari jali etc. If the farmers adopt stall feeding, then the widely propagated fear of environmentalists about these animals can be effectively met. The main problem, however, is that stall feeding may be beyond the reach of poor peasants and landless labourers and could make small ruminant rearing uneconomical and non-viable.

1.3 Review of Relevant Research Work

Not much work has been done on the socio-economic aspects of small ruminants in India. So far the focus has been on agricultural research and development. In animal husbandry also, a major share of research and developmental activities has been on large ruminants like cattle and buffaloes. Available research work on small ruminants has been reviewed here so that important research questions (issues) can be raised to be answered through our study.

Many researchers have come to the conclusion that sheep and goats play a very important role in the economy of rural households. It is argued that goats' population is increasing without any policy perspectives about them, due to their higher productivity and adaptability to any kind of situations. A large number of households are now taking up goat rearing. The erratic trend in the growth of goats' population, may be due to the sensitivity of the goats to drought as well as the equal facility with which the numbers recover during and after good rainfall years (Ahuja and Rathore, 1987). Goats are maintained in almost all types of eco-zones unlike sheep which are largely confined to either cold or hot regions. It was found in Maharashtra that while keeping sheep was confined to a particular region and, there too, to a very small proportion of rural households, keeping goats was found all over the state and more than a quarter of the total rural households keep them (Rath, 1992). It is argued that goat keeping is economical, particularly to the un-economic land holders under uncertain rainfall conditions (Kalia and Rajapurohit, 1989; Kalia, 1985). The importance of goat in the rural areas is evidenced by its unparalleled economic traits, ability to get acclimatized under diversified agro climatic conditions, unfastidious nature in choosing forage, high fertility and short generation interval, practically no religious restrictions for goat and its products among the diversified religious people in rural areas. Goats' milk appears to be nearer to human milk in nutrition, and it is believed that it has good scope in making baby food. Goat milk can yield good quality cheese. Tellichery goat's milk even have curative effects against rheumatism (Gopalakrishnan and G. M. M. Lal, 1985).

It has been brought out in the report of the task force (Government of India, 1987) that in India sheep and goats rearing was taken up mainly in those areas where for ecological reasons crop production as well as other agricultural activities have become either difficult or impossible. It is said that about 15 million people in India are partially or fully dependent on income from small ruminant related economic activities, of which more than 1/3 are rural based either engaged in rearing or wool/hair production, weaving, spinning, tanning etc. (Govt. of India, 1987). Chauhan and Moorti have pointed out in their study on Economics of Sheep

Farming in Himachal Pradesh that in India about 40 per cent of the rural population depended directly on animal husbandry particularly sheep rearing. They have also observed that sheep raising had always flourished in India, in areas with scanty and uncertain rainfall and inadequate irrigation (Chauhan and Moorti, 1990).

Acharya has shown that sheep and goats played an important role in arid, semi-arid and hilly areas where crop or dairy farming was not economical and where one could find a large number of small and marginal farmers and landless labourers (Acharya, 1984). Ivory and Semali have also observed that in general higher sheep and goat populations were found in less-intensive farming, drier regions, and upland or hilly areas that did not favour cultivation (Ivory and Semali, 1987). Jodha is of the view that in a mixed farming system where crop cultivation is uncertain and maintaining cattle is also difficult sheep and goats can be raised as supplementary source of income (Jodha, 1966).

In a study on sheep and goats in four Southern States of India-Karnataka, Kerala, Tamil Nadu and Andhra Pradesh, it has been estimated that these states accounted for about 39 per cent of the total animals slaughtered in India during 1977-78. The density of sheep and goats in South India was about 28 sheep/km^2 and about 27 goats/km^2 as against 13 sheep/km^2 and 22 goats/km^2 for the rest of the country. The study finds that small ruminant production is mainly in the hands of low-income, landless or small scale subsistence farmers who either possess no land or own holdings with low return (Mukundan and Balakrishnan, 1987).

Within complex small farm systems, even where the emphasis is on crop production, goats and sheep are found essential to the farming community and in the utilization of scarce resources (Devendra, 1987). Sheep and goats production is typically a small-scale farmer activity attracting minimum investment in housing, feed, and health care, and is, therefore, largely sustained by the potential of the indigenous breeds themselves (Hart and Knipscheer, 1987). It has been indicated in a study that in West Java the involvement of rural households in raising small ruminants was very large, that one out of every five farmers keeps sheep or goats, and participation by the farmers in this activity was as high as 30 per cent (Devendra, 1987). It has been further stated in this study that the value of small ruminants is also significant in the wider context of agroforestry systems, where the complementary advantages are forage production, supply of fuel wood, improvement of soil fertility and permanent soil cover, and economic land use.

Amir has argued in his study of goat meat production that the demand for goat meat is directly related to changes in income. Income elasticity of demand for goat meat is greater than unity. Further, in the case of goat production, profitability is not the only criteria used by the farmers. They also consider risk aversion, subsistence and family nutrition (Amir, 1988).

It has been widely accepted that rearing of sheep and goats is economical. Gross returns per household from small ruminants are substantial. Important inputs required are own family labour and dry grass, herbages, thorns etc. from waste lands and other common property resources. Ahuja and Rathore in their study on goats conducted in Ajmer and Sirohi districts of Rajasthan have concluded that goat keeping is economical in terms of milk and meat production and the only major cost component was labour, which was also provided by children and old people whose opportunity cost was low or zero. They found that in the household economy, the share of goats to total gross receipts from crop and livestock was 16.3 per cent in Ajmer and 19.2 per cent in Sirohi. Out of the total receipts from goats, the share of milk constituted 65.7 and 57.8 per cent in Ajmer and Sirohi respectively. Also, the gross receipts per goat was higher in the smallest herd size category than in the largest herd size in both Ajmer and Sirohi (Ahuja and Rathore, 1987).

It has been found in a study on the Economics of Sheep Farming in Himachal Pradesh that among the farm sources, sheep contributed the highest income on all the categories of farms. The income derived from sheep was calculated to be 43.30 per cent, 79.90 per cent, 80.07 per cent and 66.81 per cent on small, medium, large and all-farms, respectively. The sheep enterprise accounted for 87.52 per cent of the total income from crops and sheep together (Chauhan and Moorti, 1990).

The inputs used in goat rearing are almost free as the opportunity cost of labour involved in collecting these inputs is zero. With some capital investment and managerial adjustment, a small holder (one hectare of dry land) could integrate goat rearing with crop husbandry and can have a five-fold increase in his earnings (Kalia and Rajapurohit, 1989). In a study conducted by Central Arid Zone Research Institute (CAZRI, 1983) in the arid zones of India, it has been estimated that, at 1981 prices for a herd of 100 goats the fixed cost and variable cost came to Rs. 1,454 and Rs. 25,771 per annum respectively. From the sale of goats, milk, hair and manure, a gross income of Rs. 50,325 and net income of Rs. 23,100 per annum could be obtained. About two men were found to be required daily to look after the herd. Similarly, it was estimated that for a flock of 100 sheep, the fixed and variable costs came to Rs. 1,454 and Rs. 17,500 per annum respectively at 1981 prices. From the sale of sheep, wool and manure, a gross income of Rs. 38,025 and the net income of Rs. 6,146 per annum could be obtained, and two persons were found to be required to look after the flock as in the case of goats.

Keeping sheep and goats under incentive-based (production remunerative) system is more economical than raising under conventional (hired labour) system. Income under incentive-based system was 244 per cent higher than under the conventional farm managemental system (Swain *et al.* 1986). Sundaram *et al.* have estimated the cost and returns for one unit of 20 ewes and one ram, using the information collected from a few selected farmers. Net returns are worked out to be Rs. 2,700 per annum which are found to be remunerative and very much encouraging (Sundaram *et al.* 1981).

In another study, where the socio-economic conditions of a semi-nomadic upper caste family with a better off living in Rajasthan, Jodha has estimated that on an average of five years the gross returns from sheep and goats (with an initial stock of 85 goats and 200 sheep) was Rs. 3,300 per annum. Out of which almost half goes on expenditure to meet the cost of labour in the form of cash payments, food, shoes and clothes, and the cost of outmigration. The expenditure does not include the imputed value of family labour (Jodha, 1966).

In the same state of Rajasthan economics of sheep rearing has been studied by Ram and Vyas, using a different methodology. Three districts-Jaisalmer, Jodhpur and Pali have been selected for the study on the basis of highest sheep population. It has been found that economies of scale do exist in sheep rearing. The net returns in small stock holdings with an average stock strength of around 40 could generate an annual income of Rs. 4 to 10 per head. Whereas in a unit larger by nearly 3 times that of small stock holdings could generate 3 to 4 times larger income per head (Ram and Vyas, 1984).

The evaluation study on sheep rearing in Nalgonda district of Andhra Pradesh conducted by the National Bank for Agriculture and Rural Development (NABARD) has found that among the beneficiaries—for whom NABARD had financed with sheep units over a period of three years—the financial rate of return was viable and rearing sheep was much profitable. Gross income per unit during the 4th year after investment was of the order of Rs. 3,490 each for a unit size of 31 animals and Rs. 3,070 for a unit size of 21 animals. Net income without allowing for the imputed cost of family labour was Rs. 3,140, Rs. 2,950 and Rs. 2,770 from the unit size of 31, 26 and 21 animals respectively. After adjusting for the value of family labour, the net income worked out to Rs. 2,510, Rs. 2,490 and Rs. 2,770 from the flock size of 31, 26 and 21 animals, respectively (NABARD, 1982). This shows that the economic viability of a rural household is improved through supplementary income from small ruminants, even if it can be relied upon as an exclusive and the only source of income.

To analyse sheep and goat production system at the whole-farm level a linear programming approach was used by Gutierrez-Aleman in his study, a Ph.D thesis on sheep and goat production system in the Sertao region of north-east Brazil. The analysis indicated that four enterprises (crops, cattle, sheep and goats) should be included in the solution for a positive net cash income at the whole-farm level. The result also shows the tremendous influence of weather on feed production and farm income relative to an improvement of small ruminant herd/flock productivity (Gutierrez-Aleman, 1983). Singh and Swarup in their study on sheep have also found that on an average the total cost of rearing a sheep was calculated to be Rs. 89 per annum. The annual gross returns per sheep worked out to be Rs. 128. They are also of the view that economies of scale do exist in sheep rearing (Ranveer Singh and R. Swarup, 1985).

Amir's study of goat meat production in Dera Kher Muqadam in the Punjab, Pakistan, during 1987, is based on five small scale farmers with an average land holding size of 4 acres. It has shown that in goat rearing, profit over variable costs was positive as far as the farmer's perspective on cost and returns are concerned. Labour is valued much lower than it is valued by the researchers, especially the value of child labour. Also, farmers do not value wasted bread as the researchers do. On the other hand, as per the estimates made through researchers' perspective, profit over variable costs was negative (Amir, 1988). Deoghare *et al.* in their study conducted in Farah block of Mathura in Uttar Pradesh have shown that keeping small ruminants particularly, goat rearing is economical. The study was based on data collected from the rural households. In goat rearing the overall margin per household per annum over cost A was Rs. 1136, over cost B Rs. 988 and over cost C (which include imputed value of family labour) was Rs. 648. The net margin over cost A, Cost B and Cost C per Rs. 100 of investment was 38, 33 and 21 per cent respectively. Taking Cost A into account (*i.e.* all cash expenses incurred + depreciation), on an average a goat keeper having a size of 4.67 number of goats could earn about 95 rupees per month. Further in sheep rearing, the over all net returns over cost A, cost B and cost C was Rs. 2150, Rs. 2,045 and Rs. 325 respectively. The net returns over cost A, Cost B and Cost C per 100 rupees of investment was 22, 21 and 3 per cent respectively (Deoghare *et al.* 1990).

Keeping sheep and goats under any type of situations or farming system is remunerative. Devendra has reported that in Indonesia, the contribution of sheep and goat enterprise in total farming income was about 14, 17 and 26 per cent for the three categories of low land, upland and rubber plantation situations respectively. The income share of small ruminant enterprise increases as the farmer's resource base, especially land decreases (Devendra, 1987).

In the rearing of small ruminants many stock raisers give importance to manure. In Peruvian agriculture, apart from its critical role as fertilizer in crop cultivation, small ruminants' manure is used in cooking and heating as fuel. Also it is so valuable that apart from being sold and bought, it is used almost like money to pay the wages for agricultural labourers or rent on extra land taken for cropping. Even it is exchanged as a gift among relatives and friends (McCorkle *et al.* 1987).

In Kenya the dependence by the families on income from other sources tend to decline as the herd size (goats) increases. But families with well over 100 goats were still dependent on some other sources of income for at least 50 per cent of the time (Ruth Mace, 1989). In northern Tamil Nadu (India) a number of females own one or two sheep and goats. The customary shepherds (Yadhavas) whose main occupation is shepherding own 500 to 600 animals per family. By folding of sheep each shepherd gets around Rs. 8 per night with one full meal. Further, a shepherd with 50 animals estimated his average monthly income at around Rs. 100, which is above the average income of most of the small farmers and labourers (John Harriss, 1982).

Even in areas where commercial crops like sugarcane is grown, keeping sheep and goats as a subsidiary source of income is advisable. In a survey of goat-sesbania relations in Maharashtra, it has been shown that, income from an average goat unit of 6 in the irrigated sugarcane belt (goat-sesbania zone) varies from Rs. 800 to Rs. 1,200 per household, whereas it hardly varies from Rs. 400 to Rs. 600 in the adjoining dry areas (Acacia Zone). In the irrigated sugarcane belt farmers grow sesbania trees as shelter belts on bunds which are assured source of fodder to the goats the whole year. Further, twinning (two kids per birth) among goats was 60 per cent in the sesbania zone as compared with the adjoining non-sesbania areas, where it was hardly 20 per cent (Gopalkirshnan and G.M.M Lal, 1985).

Small ruminants are kept as security against risk. Farmers keep these animals as their assets, which can be converted into cash at any time. The socio-economic status of the rural households is often assessed on the basis of assets they possess which include sheep and goats also. The value of goats per household was accounted for 27.9 and 31.2 per cent of the value of livestock assets of the sample households in Ajmer and Sirohi respectively (Ahuja and Rathore, 1987). In a study based on the multi disciplinary research project supported by the U.S. Congress and in operation in five less developed countries: Brazil, Indonesia, Kenya, Moracco and Peru, it has been argued that for many less developed countries small ruminants are valued not so much for their yield of animal products and cash, as for their role in households overall survival strategy. Small ruminants are only one component within larger complex system of resource and risk management. In Brazil the small holders keep goats mainly as a low cost hedge against drought and to supply basic family needs like meat and cash during such difficult periods. They devote little time, capital, veterinary or other care to the goats which they largely manage on their own (McCorkle *et al.* 1987).

It is more advantageous to keep goats and sheep as compared with other domestic ruminants like cattle and buffaloes. Particularly so to the poor and landless households with poor resource base. Households with very low level of inputs like capital and fodder can keep sheep and goats for subsistence. It is also easy to maintain sheep and goats and they are less harmful to environment and trees than cattle or buffaloes. It has been found that in the case of cattle, fodder requirement per animal is 2 1/2 to 3 times more than required per sheep or goat (Govt. of India, 1987). Unlike a cow, a few goats can be maintained more easily and can be disposed of at no great loss in years of drought (Rath, 1992).

Goat produces 185 kgs milk per 100 kg digestible organic matter as compared with cow, which produces 162 kgs milk per 100 kg digestible organic matter. Unlike cow, goat is almost 100 per cent efficient in converting feed carotene into vitamin A. Where feed is scarce and of low nutritive value, cattle and buffaloes are at a disadvantage because of their high maintenance requirements (Shankarnarayan *et al.* 1985). It has also been shown that in the indigenous cow enterprise, the net margin per household per annum over cost C (cost C include imputed value of family labour) was negative for all types of farmers, whereas in the case of goats and sheep it was positive (Deoghare, *et al.* 1990). The nutrient conversion efficiency for milk production of a dairy cow is on an average 38 per cent, whereas for goat it ranges between 45 and 71 per cent. It is also recorded that goats are 4.4 per cent superior to sheep, 7.9 per cent to buffaloes and 8.6 per cent to cows in crude fibre utilisation. Kidding among goats is twice in 14 months and a single doe produces seven female kids in eight years, which cannot be achieved either by a cow or a buffalo in their life period (Gopalakrishnan and G.M.M. Lal, 1985).

Under natural range land system, raising indigenous sheep and goats seem to be remunerative and advisable. Particularly in the semi-arid regions under free range grazing/browsing on degraded grazing lands, indigenous breeds of small ruminants are more suitable to cross-bred animals. The indigenous purebred goats were superior to the cross-bred by 101 per cent and indigenous sheep to cross-bred by 89.6 per cent. Higher returns from indigenous animals could be attributed to their higher fecundity, low mortality resulting in disposal of more animals and high nutrient digestibility resulting in good animal performance (Swain *et al.* 1986).

Deforestation is often blamed on small ruminants. But sheep and goats never go to the grown up trees. Erosion and compaction of soil and exploitation of phytomas is almost 3 to 5 times more due to cattle as compared with sheep and goats. Within the desired grazing pressure, sheep and goats are more economical and less harmful than large ruminants (Govt. of India, 1987).

Yet, small ruminants, particularly goats, are subject to severe criticisms as the destroyers of vegetation, which it is argued has been vastly exaggerated. As Rath has pointed out that the sheep and goats, particularly the latter, are responsible for degradation of forest and other common land has been an unstated or stated assumption for too long (Rath, 1992). The goat does cause destruction to the environment but only when it is raised with lack of controlled management (Devendra and Mcleroy, 1982). Further, it is argued that sheep and goats do not pose a threat to the ecology as is generally believed. If the attention is focused exclusively on the negative aspects to reduce the number of sheep and goats, ecological damage is almost certain to occur, because it would be a near impossibility to restrict their numbers through administrative action in the face of the strong economic logic favouring an increase in their numbers. Ecological imbalance can thus arise in the absence of positive measures to improve the carrying capacity of land (Government of India, 1987).

Based on the literature reviewed in this chapter, important research issues are raised in the next chapter to be addressed in the subsequent chapters.

2

OBJECTIVES AND METHODOLOGY

2.1 Objectives of the Study

Though small ruminants can play a significant role in the economies of rural households and particularly in the economies of poor peasants and landless households in the droughtprone regions, no significant efforts have been made on the development and management of these animals. Our literature review also reveals this fact. It is further important to concentrate on these animals, keeping in view the anti-poverty programmes, where in poor peasants and landless families have to be supported with viable and sustainable assets through loans and subsidies, so that they can cross the poverty line. Since sheep and goats are manageable by all types of households, it is essential to understand the role played by these animals in the economies of rural households for further policy implications. Economics of small ruminants is studied here, not in the narrow perspective of private business economics of a firm or household, but in broader terms including not only economic viability and efficiency, but also inter-class differences, social costs and environmental considerations. Rearing sheep and goats may be advantageous to those rural households with an easy and assured access to inputs like labour, capital and fodder. Rich households may have capital and land but may lack own labour. On the other hand, poor and landless may have abundant labour but may lack land and capital. Further, small ruminants are maintained mostly on public lands including the CPRs, for which the individuals have to pay nothing. But the social costs in terms of deforestation, land degradation and soil erosion etc. as a result of unplanned grazing is borne by the society, which may also have an adverse environmental impact on the ecology of the region.

The economics of small ruminants would be studied mainly through three dimensions-efficiency including capacity for survival in the face of risk, sustainability and equity, which are also very closely inter-related.

As the droughtprone regions are subject to severe stresses like crop failures and unemployment, it is of particular importance to study how the rural households, especially the poor and landless, respond to such crises by keeping these animals; the extent to which small ruminants help the rural population in diversifying their risk; and the extent of dependence of different classes on these animals during such periods. We have to see in particular whether rearing of small ruminants makes poor peasants and landless households more sensitive to droughts, or on the contrary enables them to survive from droughts better. In this connection, it is proposed to study the costs and returns in the rearing of small ruminants across different class of rural households and across different flock sizes.

The relationship between economics of small ruminants and village environment has to be probed at the aggregative level of the village, but the interaction can be studied at the household level too. Small ruminants production depends to a greater extent on forages, herbages and grasses from range lands and common property resources (CPRs), it is worth understanding the relationships between range lands, CPRs and small ruminant production, particularly from the point of view of the growing concern of degradation of these lands by the grazing of small ruminants. Small ruminants rearing may come in the way of developmental programmes like social forestry and integrated development of watersheds, by way of their grazing and management practices. Though it is generally believed that small ruminants and particularly goats are harmful to vegetation, we would like to probe into apart from the economics of small ruminants, whether rearing small ruminants really affects the environment, and in which case how the rural households, across classes and castes, manage to keep these animals. The social costs of small ruminants rearing could be different from the private costs, where there is dependence on common property resources. While studying these aspects, we would also like to see if there are institutional arrangements in the villages to make the small ruminant economy sustainable in the long run. There is a fear that in the absence of controlled grazing, small ruminants can easily out compete with cattle and cause deforestation. Damodaran has pointed out that this has been to the disadvantage of the poor sections, since the poor tend to prefer keeping cattle to small ruminants (Damodaran, 1987). We have to see if this is valid in other places too. We would like to investigate the importance of common property resources (CPRs) in the rearing of small ruminants. In the absence of CPRs for grazing, is it possible to maintain small ruminants on stall feeding? The fear is that degradation of CPRs or their disappearance may not very much harm the privileged sections of the rural society, who can afford to produce or purchase the fodder needed by them. The poor and landless, however, may have to forego even this last resort of income and employment. It is of particular importance to investigate and understand how far the rearing of sheep and goats is helpful in maintaining the sustainability of the droughtprone or semi-arid regions.

It has been hypothesised that rearing of small ruminants brings equity across different classes of rural households. The equity or distributional aspect is related to finding out if indeed economies of scale exist favouring large holders, or even if they exist whether there is a threshold of viability below which it is uneconomical to rear small ruminants. Small ruminants and crop cultivation have certain complementarities. The rich farmers may concentrate on crop cultivation due to their access to land and capital, whereas the poor peasants and landless may concentrate on small ruminants rearing which can be maintained on own labour, the only surplus input of these classes. The manure of small ruminants raised by the poor and landless brings some returns to them from the rich farmers both directly in the farm of cash through sales as well as indirectly through stubble grazing. It is preferred in crop cultivation as a very good fertilizer and hence the big farmers prefer to buy it on cash. Also, the big holders allow the small ruminants of the poor and landless to graze on their fields after the crop is harvested, so that their land gets enriched through the droppings of small ruminants in the field. Understanding this particular system which brings equity across classes in the rural society is of utmost relevance. In the present day monetized village economy, the big holders may themselves use the stubbles for their own livestock intensively. It is thus proposed here to study the size and composition of different ruminant livestock across castes and classes and the causes behind the changes in the stock if any, and to find what role the small ruminants play in the economy of different classes of rural households both in income and employment generation.

It is also intended to study the marketing aspects of small ruminants and their products at the household and at the village level. The marketing problems may also have an impact on the cost and returns from small ruminants. It is necessary to find how far the small ruminant keepers are subject to exploitation by middlemen and traders. Different types of constraints may come in the way of sheep and goats producers in realising the full potential of the market for their produce, which again may make the small ruminant economy less economical.

2.2 Study Area and Selection of the Villages

Since it is proposed to study the economics of small ruminants in a droughtprone region of Karnataka, we had to identify a fairly representative semi-arid region with a significant small ruminant economy. The droughtprone talukas in each district have been listed by the Irrigation Commission (1972). Based on this, the droughtprone districts, non-droughtprone districts and mixed type of districts in Karnataka have been identified (Nadkarni, 1985). The classification was based on whether the bulk of the taluks (55 % and above) within each district were droughtprone. Districts with less than 55 per cent of talukas as droughtprone were classified as mixed, and those where no talukas are droughtprone were treated as non-droughtprone. After listing the droughtprone districts, we have calculated the density of small ruminants per sq.km. in each district as well as the number of small ruminants per 100 rural households. Kolar ranks first in the state in terms of small ruminants per 100 rural households and second in terms of density of small ruminants per sq. km. (see Table, 2.1). Though Mandya ranks first in terms of small ruminants per sq. km., it is a mixed type of district with a high proportion of area under irrigation. On the other hand, Kolar is a droughtprone region with a low level of irrigation[1]. Since our interest is mainly in the role of small ruminants in droughtprone regions, we have selected Kolar district as our study region. Incidentally it may be noted from Table 2.1 that the droughtprone and mixed districts show much higher levels of small ruminants per sq.km. and also per 100 rural households. We shall, however, discuss more on this in the next chapter.

Following the same procedure, we selected Bagepalli taluka for the detailed study. Bagepalli is a dry taluka with mostly rainfed agriculture, with hill slopes, barren and marginal lands in Kolar district. We find highest density of small ruminants per sq. km. and the highest number of small ruminants per

1. The proportion of gross irrigated area to gross cropped area was 24.5 per cent and 43.4 per cent in Kolar and Mandya districts respectively.

100 rural households here (Table 2.1). Further, in Bagepalli taluka we have selected a cluster of three villages—Achepalli, Neergantpalli and Gurraldinne, purposively, where we find a large concentration of small ruminants with a relatively lower level of agricultural activities and a large proportion of farmers living on rainfed agriculture. With the help of a brief structured questionnaire basic data on land utilization, population, different species of livestock, sources of irrigation, sources of income etc. was collected on census basis from all the 285 households in the selected villages. Thus, a total of 102 households with small ruminants were identified, which form the basis for our detailed investigation. A structured questionnaire was used for detailed investigation, supplemented by informal interviews. Before Collecting the household data, the questionnaire was pre-tested in Bagepalli taluka in different villages.

Detailed household data were collected for one year period from April 1987 to March 1988. Since most of the does/Ewes in the herd/flock kid/lamb once in a year during February/ March, it was much easier to collect the correct data on organic increase and cost and returns from goats and sheep from April to March. Field work was carried on during four months from March to June, 1988. The reasons for choosing this period for field work were: Firstly, it was an off season from the point of view of crop cultivation for most of the dry farming households and hence easy to get the respondents; and secondly, to observe and understand the village environment and the grazing system of ruminants during the dry season.

Apart from the quantitative information through questionnaires, information was recorded through observation, participation and discussion with the village elders. In understanding the type and composition of ruminants, condition of the grazing lands and particularly common property land resources (CPRs), management and institutional arrangements of CPRs, both at present as well as in the past, discussion with the village elders were very useful.

Table 2.1

Small Ruminants in Karnataka State and Kolar District

Districts	*Karnataka State* No. of Small Ruminants		*Taluks*	*Kolar District* No. of Small Ruminants	
	Per Km²	*Per 100 Rural Households*		*Per Km²*	*Per 100 Rural Households*
Droughtprone Districts					
Bangalore	78.7	202.8	Bagepalli	120.5	509.3
Bellary	48.7	277.2	Bangarpet	116.1	345.0
Bijapur	54.5	303.9	Chikballapur	92.5	341.2
Chitradurga	70.5	333.7	Chintamani	102.2	343.9
Gulbarga	44.5	249.3	Gouribidnur	110.0	282.8
Kolar	107.4	348.1	Malur	118.3	349.3
Mysore	43.9	154.6	Kolar	108.9	302.3
Raichur	46.0	244.2	Mulbagal	101.7	343.4
Tumkur	88.1	300.0	Sidlaghatta	101.2	336.3
			Srinivasapur	97.7	378.0
			Kolar District	107.4	348.1
Non-Droughtprone Districts					
Bidar	32.0	125.0			
Coorg	2.8	14.5			
Chikmaglur	18.8	100.5			
Dakshina Kannada	3.6	10.5			
Shimoga	15.5	80.0			
Uttara Kannada	2.3	17.4			
Mixed Districts					
Belgaum	64.0	223.6			
Dharwar	37.7	167.4			

Hassan	53.7	181.9
Madhya	109.9	260.9
State	48.7	205.0

Source: Based on the data from:

1. 13th Livestock Census, 1983, Department of Animal Husbandry and Veterinary Services, Government of Karnataka, Bangalore, 1985.
2. Census of India, 1981 Series-9, Karnataka, Part II-B (1): Primary Census Abstract, General Population, 1984.
3. Census of India, 1981 Series-9, Karnataka, Paper 4 of 1984, Occupied Residential Houses and Households.

2.3 Methodology and Study Design

The economics of small ruminants has been studied mainly from the point of individual households as decision making units in terms of their self-interest. But this has also been supplemented by an analysis of the natural and marketing environment faced by these households and the interaction between the household economy and the village environment. The methodology is therefore designed towards this end, requiring an analysis of both the household level data and the village level environment. The latter has been probed informally within the village and the neighbourhood to form qualitative judgments. While the methodology follows the neo-classical approach to production economics at the micro level, our approach has also taken into account how this economics of small ruminants is differentiated by the rural class structure. Rural households may keep small ruminants as an hedge against risk in their total household economies. They may not calculate the cost of their own labour as well as free inputs used in the rearing of sheep and goats. Only those households with surplus and/or unused inputs, whose opportunity costs are zero or negligible, may keep small ruminants.

There are more than one criteria of classifying rural

households. Size of holdings by themselves do not have much analytical significance, since holdings are not comparable and their standardisation is rather difficult due to the differences in cropping system, soil condition, extent of irrigation etc. Moreover, we cannot be even definite that these factors are exogenous to size of holding or are influenced by it. We have preferred to classify the rural households into different classes taking into account the rural labour participation in agriculture. Bardhan has classified the rural households into five classes using the criterion of labour utilization in agriculture, *i.e.* self employment (SE), hired in (HI) and hired out (HO) labour (Bardhan; 1982)[2]. We have departed a little from Bardhan and have classified the rural households with small ruminants into three different class groups instead of five. There were no landlords with zero self-employment in our sample. All classes had used some own labour, not merely for management but also for physical work. With all classes having self-employment greater than zero, the class of rich peasants is taken by us to be those depending mainly on hired in labour, there being no question of hiring out labour. The rest of the rural households are all poor, but unlike in Bardhan's classification where he assumes zero hired-in labour, there were no households here which did not at all hire-in some labour. This was so particularly because of animal husbandry, where some hiring-in of labour is in evidence in almost all households. The criterion for poor households is that they hire out more labour than hire-in. But among them, we make a further classification into *(i)* poor peasants with some land, and *(ii)* landless labour without any cultivated land (ignoring homestead land not used for proper cultivation except raising one or two trees). Further, hired

2. Bardhan's classification of rural households:
   1. Landlords : SE = 0, HI > 0, HO = 0
   2. Capitalist farmers : SE > 0, HI > 0, HO = 0
   3. Family farmers : SE > 0, HI = 0, HO = 0
   4. Small farmers : SE > 0, HI = 0, HO = 0
   5. Landless labour : SE > 0, HI = 0, HO > 0.

labour in the case of landless labour is negligible in relation to hired out labour, whereas it was a little more significant in the case of poor peasants. But this is relative difference and our criterion is not dependent on this. Thus our classes are:

Class	*Criteria*
Rich peasants (RP)	Hired out labour = 0
	Hired in labour >0
	Cultivated Land > 0
Poor Peasants (PP)	Hired out labour > Hired in labour
	Cultivated land > 0
Landless Labour (LL)	Hired out labour > Hired in labour
	Cultivated land = 0

It has to be noted that the prefix 'rich' applied to peasants does not indicate absolute richness. They are called 'rich' only because they happen to employers, and cannot be compared the urban rich or rich as we popularly think of. Perhaps the term, non-poor may be more suitable, but they are certainly richer than the other two classes. We are hesitant to call them as 'capitalist' peasants because most of them do not posses costly capital assets like tractors. They are, however, capitalist in so far as they employ some labour.

The above classification has been on the basis of the total household economy including both agriculture and livestock including small ruminants. However, hiring out of labour for salaried jobs and for non-agricultural activities like mining has been ignored in classifying the rural households.

Out of the total 285 households covered through census in the three cluster villages of Bagepalli taluka, 35.9 per cent possess small ruminants. The percentage of households with small ruminants to total households in each selected village represents more or less the same proportion, *viz.* Achepalli 36.4 per cent, Neergantpalli 33.7 per cent and Gurraldinne 39.0 per cent. We have clubbed all the households with small ruminants of the three villages which comes to a total of 102 households for further analysis.

Thus we have categorised the three classes of households with small ruminants as follows:

1. Rich Peasants

There are 37 relatively rich peasant households who depend on hired labour apart from own or family labour for crop cultivation and animal husbandry. There is no hiring out of any labour in this group. There are two households with teaching as their main occupation with less than five acres of land. Since their annual income is on par with the rich peasants, we have included them in this category. Land holding size of households in this group is above five acres, including irrigated land. We have classified this group of households as rich peasants, to have a comparison over other peasants. They are not rich as compared with the households in an irrigated village.

2. Poor Peasants

We have 61 households in this category, who are depending both for crop cultivation and animal husbandry, mostly on own labour with or without some hired in labour. But they hire-out their labour substantially, *i.e.*, they live on wage earnings also. Though they also hire-in some labour, it is less than labour hired out. There was, however, one household which neither hired-in nor hired-out labour, the family size being very small and its main occupation being small ruminants rearing. The household has been included in this category as it has some land even if meagre, *viz.*, 0.25 acres of dry land. There are many very poor households in this category, their standard of living and income levels being more or less equal to the landless households. In order to get a financial benefit from a voluntary organisation reserved for cultivators, they have encroached on the hill slopes (ranging from 0.25 to 1.00 acre) and have reported as land owners. But in practice they do not have the 'patta' on the encroached land and get practically nothing or very marginal output from such lands. Since they are cultivating some land even if encroached and uneconomical, we have included them in this category.

3. Landless Labour

There were only four households in this group. There were of course other landless labour households, but they didn't have small ruminants. The households with small ruminants possessed some homestead land for living and for keeping their livestock, but no cultivable land. They mainly depended on wage earnings through hiring out labour, supplementing their income with animal husbandry. Though these households could be combined with the poor peasants, we have kept them separate to see whether there is any variation in terms of gross and net returns from small ruminants between the two groups. That would bring out the importance of possessing some cultivable land, even if meagre.

To have a comparison of certain basic socio-economic characteristics between the households with small ruminants and households without small ruminants we have also classified the latter across different classes. Since no detailed survey was undertaken for households without small ruminants, we do not have the data for labour utilization in agriculture and animal husbandry of these households. We had to use our judgement based on the survey of households with small ruminants, to have corresponding classes among these households. We have taken the land holding size of the last household listed on the descending order in the rich peasant class of households with small ruminants as the cut off point to classify the rich peasant class among the households without small ruminants. This cut-off point turned to be 5 acres of dry land. Households with below five acres of land have been categorised as poor peasants. Thus we have classified the households without small ruminants as follows:

1. *Rich Peasants* : with 5 acres of dry land and above[3]
2. *Poor Peasants* : with Less than 5 acres of dry land
3. *Landless Labour* : with no cultivable land

The data have been analysed in two ways, across class of farmers and across size of flock/herd. To know the cost and returns, viability and the constraints faced by the different classes of agricultural households, the data have been classified across classes. On the other hand, to examine the economies of scale to different class of farmers, the same data have been analysed across different size of flocks, so that we can understand about the viable units of small ruminants. To have an integrated view, we shall also see which classes of households keep which size of flock/herd.

The study is based both on secondary as well as primary data. Secondary data have been collected for the variables like total ruminant livestock population (species wise), geographical area, grazing lands etc., at the national, state and for Karnataka at the district level. Primary data are based on the field work carried in the villages of a typically droughtprone district of Karnataka. Our approach here rest both on a study of village level information including its common property resources (CPRs) that sustain livestock, and also on the basis of a detailed survey of the households which keep small ruminants. The census listing of all households in the village covered information on size of holdings, the number of family members and their work or occupational status and the type, and number and type of livestock with them. Though the listing was done primarily to identify households which keep small ruminants, the information has been analysed for

3. We have standardised the land holdings as one acre of irrigated land is equal to three acres of dry land, taking the gross returns per acre in both the cases for arriving at this equivalence.

other purposes too, mainly to know distribution of livestock population by types across different classes of rural households and the other sources of income to the households without small ruminants. Apart from structured questionnaires used both for listing and the detailed survey, informal discussions and interviews have been employed for recording other relevant information.

The study is also based on information and insights gathered from several other villages in different districts of Karnataka. Through extensive field work in rural Karnataka (as part of other research work), information gathered on the socio-economic aspects of small ruminant keepers in different agro-economic and environmental conditions, grazing systems, contribution of small ruminants to total household income, use and management of common property resources (CPRs) in the rearing of sheep and goats etc. has been used.

The Concepts of Costs and Returns Used

The Concepts of Costs

To arrive at net returns we have to calculate the gross returns and costs from agriculture and animal husbandry during the reference year. We have followed the cost concepts used in agriculture by the Farm Management Studies and cost of cultivation surveys. Studies on costs of cultivation in agriculture were launched during the 1950s and four cost concepts were used. They were:

A1 = All actual expenses in cash and kind incurred by owner operator;

A2 = Cost A1 + rent paid for leased-in land;

B = Cost A2 + rental value of owned land (net of land revenue) and interest on owned fixed capital excluding land;

C = Cost B + imputed value of family labour.

Since imputed rent was actually a surplus and not a cost, an expert committee chaired by Professor S. R. Sen suggested modification to this scheme so that imputed rent on owned land could be separated. The revised cost concepts suggested by this committee which are now in vogue are:

A1 = All actual expenses in cash and kind incurred by owner operator;

A2 = Cost A1 + rent paid for leased-in land;

B1 = Cost A1+ interest on value of owned capital assets (excluding land);

B2 = Cost B1 + rental value of owned land (net of land revenue);

C1 = Cost B1 + imputed value of family labour;

C2 = Cost B2+ imputed value of family labour.

We have adopted the above cost concepts in our study with some modification. The rental value of owned land has not been taken, both because theoretically it is a part of surplus rather than a cost as such, and also because estimation of imputed rent in an area where tenancy is not prominent can be arbitrary. But we had also to go further in animal husbandry to accommodate two more costs—cost on account of risk bearing and social costs.

The cost concepts used by us for crop cultivation which correspond to traditional concepts, are:

Cost A1 = All paid out cost (cash and kind), value of own Bullock days used, value of own Farm Yard Manure (FYM) and seeds, Transportation and other miscellaneous expenses;

Cost A2 = Cost A1 + rent paid for leased-in land;

Cost B1 = A2 + interest on owned capital assets (excluding land);

Cost C1 = B1 + imputed value of family labour;

We have adopted the same cost concepts in animal

husbandry also, with some more costs into it. Thus cost A1 would include the cost of own and purchased fodder. Cost C1 is a private cost, *i.e.*, from the point of households, even while applying it to animal husbandry. We have introduced one more cost here, i.e, cost on account of risk premium (Cr). Since in animal husbandry farmers face the loss regularly as also suffer a heavy loss during abnormal years. Loss during the normal years is largely due to the death of animals, low returns through sale and due to predators. The loss during abnormal years is mainly due to large scale epidemics which swallow a large part of the stock. We have estimated a risk premium and added it to cost C1 to arrive at cost Cr. The estimate is based on the information provided by the villagers as well as the veterinary officials. It has been reported that on an average heavy loss (around 15 per cent of the stock value) in the rearing of goats and sheep occurs once in five years. By distributing the loss of abnormal year (15 per cent) over 5 years, the risk premium during each year could be around 3 per cent. Thus we have estimated a risk premium of 3 per cent per annum on the average value of the stock in the beginning and at the end of the year.

Moreover, since in animal husbandry, a substantial part of total cost constitute the fodder cost, as also a substantial and in some cases almost all the fodder requirement of ruminants is met through free grazing, another cost concept has been included as Cs, *i.e.*, the imputed value of free grazing, which is nothing but the social cost. It is estimated taking into account the quantity of biomass grazed by goats and sheep on CPRs during one year period. It has been reported by the veterinary officials that on free range grazing, on an average, goats and sheep consume dry matter equivalent to 3 per cent of their body weight per day. Taking the average body weight of a live animal at 25 kgs., we have thus imputed the quantity of fodder grazed by small ruminants. Fodder so consumed is valued at Rs.100 per tonne. Since the dry matter grazed by goats and sheep on CPRs had no market value and which is much lower in quality as compared with the crop residues or other commercial fodder, it has been valued at 50 per cent of the market value of crop residues of coarse cereals in the sample villages. This is based on what goats and sheep keepers reported as their willingness to pay for fodder if free grazing was not available. Lambs and kids up to the age of 3 months are excluded while estimating the imputed value of grazing by goats and sheep.

We have used one more cost concept, Br, which comprises of Cost B1 and risk premium alone, but excludes imputed value of own labour and social cost. One could argue that there is no strong justification for including cost of own labour imputed at prevailing wage rates if its opportunity cost is zero or if its marginal value product is less than unity (i.e., if an additional input of a rupee worth of own labour at market wages brings forth less than a rupee worth of output). Such an inclusion of imputed cost may not be meaningful to poor peasants and landless labour, and may only serve to give an inflated appearance to their cost, and to imply that it is too costly for them to have small ruminants. But considering cost B1 alone is not enough, since poor peasants and landless labour too have to cover their risks in the long run.

Thus, the cost concepts used by us in animal husbandry are:

Cost A1 = All paid out cost (cash and kind), value of own fodder used, transportation and other miscellaneous expenses;

Cost A2 = A1 + rent paid on share cropping;

Cost B1[4] = A2 + interest on owned capital assets (livestock) excluding land;

---

4. Imputed interest on the average value of the stock in the beginning and at the end of the year is included in the cost, since this is what the animal keepers would have had to pay if they had to borrow money to purchase their livestock. We did not use the market rate of interest since it includes elements of risk cover and exploitation.

Cost Br = B1 + risk premium;

Cost C1 = B1 + imputed value of family labour;

Cost Cr = C1 + risk premium;

Cost Cs = Cr + imputed value of free grazing (social cost).

Own labour has been imputed on the basis of actual labour hours spent converted to standardised labour-days in a year. Total number of male and female labour days in a year are multiplied by Rs. 8 and Rs. 6 respectively (average prevailing wage rate in the sample villages per labour day of males and females respectively) to arrive at the total value of own labour days. In the case of labour hired in for animal husbandry, total wages paid in cash, value of clothes provided and imputed value of food given per year have been taken into account. Many households have hired in labour and paid wages in kind in the form of lambs, kids, etc. In such cases we have taken their imputed value (at prevailing prices in the villages).

In agriculture, labour used annually in fencing has also been included. As most of the cultivating schedule caste (land owners) households are getting Rs. 9 per day per person in each household for about five months, both as an incentive to work on their own land and also as help during dry periods from a voluntary organisation, such labour has been taken as hired out labour.

Gross Returns from Agriculture During the Year

It includes cash received through the actual sale of total output and crop residues during the year; and imputed value of output and fodder (at the prevailing rate in the village) both kept as stock and consumed at source.

The concept of Gross Returns during a year in Animal Husbandry

Gross returns here is inclusive of input costs such as feed,

We considered 10 per cent as a reasonable level of interest; otherwise, we would have very much inflated the costs, particularly because all animal keepers do not borrow money to purchase all their livestock.

labour, medicine, interest etc., which have to be deducted to arrive at net returns. Gross return is the net change in value of the stock, net proceeds from sales (after deducting expenditure on sale), value of consumed animals, and other returns. Net change in the value of the stock (NC) is St1-St0, where St1=value of the stock at the year end and St0=value of the stock at the beginning of the year. The net change in the value of stock during the year consists mainly of natural or organic growth of animals, but changes due to purchase and sale of animals and death of animals also get reflected in it. If the net change is positive, it indicates investment; if negative, it indicates disinvestment. This investment is a part of the gross returns, since current investment is a part of current income. To this we have also to add net proceeds from sale of animals and other returns.

Thus we have derived the gross returns as follows:

$$GR = NC + TS - P + CS + RD + OR$$

Where : NC = Net change in the value of the stock;

TS = Total proceeds from sale of animals;

P = Expenditure on purchase of animals;

CS = Consumption of animals at source;

RD = Returns from dead animals;

OR = Other returns (value of manure, wool, milk, skin etc.).

It may be clarified that we have excluded the value of by-products from CS like skin which is included in OR. Also, RD does not include returns from animals slaughtered for home consumption. RD reflects returns from sale of deceased animals which died of illness or due to attack by predators. As such, we have avoided double counting in the estimation of gross return from animal husbandry.

3

ROLE OF SMALL RUMINANTS IN INDIA AND KARNATAKA ECONOMY WITH SPECIAL REFERENCE TO DROUGHTPRONE AREAS

3.1 Contribution of Small Ruminants to National and State Economy

Animal husbandry occupies an important place in the Indian economy. Apart from the urban demand for milk, meat, skins and wool, almost all the rural population depend directly or indirectly on animal husbandry. It directly contributes five to six per cent of India's national income. Goats in India contribute nearly 34 per cent (244 million kgs) of total meat production, 2.7 per cent (0.7 million tonnes) of total milk production, 35 million skin pieces, 300 tonnes of hair and 50 million tonnes of dung annually, thereby contributing about 400 crores of rupees towards national income. Further, the production potential of sheep is estimated to be around Rs.140 crores per annum. This include about 34.5 million kgs. of wool, 101 million kg of mutton, 14.6 million pieces of skin and 20 million tonnes of manure (Gopalakrishnan and G.M.M. Lal, 1985).

India is one among the important countries in the world which produce goats and sheep. During 1997, 5.3 and 17 per cent of the total world population of sheep and goats, respectively, was found in India. Out of the total population of sheep and goats in the Asian continent, 13.6 per cent of sheep and 25.9 per cent of goats were found in the country. At the global level, India's share of sheep and goats meat production to total meat production from sheep and goats was 6 per cent, whereas in Asia it was 10.7 per cent during the same period. Also, both at the global level as well as in the Asian continent, Indian goats' contribution of milk to total goat milk production was substantial, being 20.44 and 36.3 per cent, respectively. In terms of wool production (both greezy and scoured), India's share to total wool production was marginal *viz.*, 1.9 per cent, at the world level, while in Asia it was 7 per cent. Further, out of the total production of sheep and goats skins in the world as well as in Asia, India's share was 7.5 and 13.8 per cent, respectively (F.A.O, 1997).

Export of small ruminant meat amounts to 0.21 per cent of total production of small ruminant meat in India. Export of processed woolen goods is earning more than 300 crores of rupees. India is among the four countries which are producing 'Gless Kid' leather—a most sought after leather in the international market (India, Government of, 1987).

In total meat production of the nation, the share of sheep and goats meat is substantial. It constituted around 48 per cent of total meat production in India as compared with around 27 per cent share of beef and buffalo meat production. Sheep and goats together play a relatively important role in Karnataka, particularly the former. The State ranked 4th in sheep meat production in India, contributing 10 per cent of total sheep meat production in the country. In goat meat production it stood 10th by contributing around 5 per cent to total goat meat production (Singh, *et al.*1990). The demand for sheep and goats in Karnataka is increasing at a very rapid rate. Number of small ruminants slaughtered for meat has increased to a large extent. The share of mutton and goat meat to total meat production was 66 per cent during 1978-79 and which has gone up to 70 per cent during 1995-96. On the other hand the share of beef and buffalo meat to total meat production which was around 31 per cent during 1978-79, came down to 25 per cent during 1995-96. Further, between 1978-79 and 1995-96 total mutton and goat meat production has increased by more than 600 per cent. Production of beef and buffalo meat too has increased by about 400 per cent during the same period (Table 3.1).

Further, at the all India level the share of livestock output (minus cost of livestock feed) in the Gross Domestic Product (GDP) has increased from 2.8 per cent to 4.9 per cent during 1970-71 to 1986-87. For Karnataka it has increased from 0.9 per cent to around 8 per cent during the period 1970-71 to 1996-97. This increase, in contrast with the fall in the share of agriculture to Gross Domestic Product, is worth noticing. Both at the all India level as well as for Karnataka, the share of agriculture (including livestock) to GDP has declined from 45.7 per cent to 24.4 per cent and from 48.4 per cent to 30 per cent, respectively, during the same period. Within the agricultural sector the value of livestock output in India constitutes 25 per cent of the total output from agriculture during 1986-87. For Karnataka, the share of the value of livestock output in the agricultural sector was 19.9 per cent during 1986-87, which has further increased to 26.6 per cent during 1996-97. In fact it has increased substantially both at the all India level as well as in Karnataka, over a period of time (see Table 3.2 below).

Table 3.1
Estimated Production and Average Price of Meat in Karnataka

Year	Production of Meat (100' tonnes)						Average Price of Meat (Rs./Kg)		
	Cattle	Buffaloes	Sheep	Goats	Pigs	Total	Small Ruminants	Large Ruminants	Pigs
1	*2*	*3*	*4*	*5*	*6*	*7*	*8*	*9*	*10*
1978-79	17.70 (15.7)	17.17 (15.2)	43.96 (38.9)	30.65 (27.1)	3.45 (3.1)	112.93 (100)	25.00	6.50	11.00
1979-80	23.37 (23.0)	12.42 (12.2)	40.44 (39.8)	20.40 (20.1)	5.05 (5.0)	101.68 (100)	26.00	6.50	12.00
1980-81	18.99 (11.0)	15.89 (9.2)	76.81 (44.5)	55.53 (32.1)	5.58 (3.2)	172.80 (100)	27.50	7.00	13.00
1981-82	30.62 (16.4)	9.41 (5.0)	79.14 (42.4)	62.82 (33.7)	4.61 (2.5)	186.60 (100)	28.00	7.00	13.50
1982-83	24.55 (10.3)	13.06 (5.5)	101.63 (42.7)	93.89 (39.4)	5.09 (2.1)	238.22 (100)	28.50	7.50	14.00
1983-84	25.90 (9.1)	10.93 (3.8)	129.52 (45.5)	112.97 (39.7)	5.40 (2.1)	284.72 (100)	29.00	8.00	14.25

(Contd.)

(Contd.)

1	2	3	4	5	6	7	8	9	10
1984-85	27.63	17.14	133.66	120.54	6.12	305.09	30.00	8.00	15.00
	(91.)	(5.6)	(43.8)	(39.5)	(2.0)	(100)			
1985-86	27.35	18.28	133.20	125.47	6.87	311.17	30.00	8.50	15.50
	(8.8)	(5.9)	(42.8)	(40.3)	(2.2)	(100)			
1986-87	29.88	19.87	144.57	155.89	7.39	357.70	31.00	8.50	16.00
	(8.4)	(5.6)	(40.4)	(43.6)	(2.1)	(100)			
1987-88	89.66	81.76	266.92	205.66	35.86	679.86	90.00	30.00	45.00
	(13.2)	(12.0)	(39.3)	(30.3)	(5.3)	(100)			

Note: Total meat production include meat from Cattle, Buffaloes, Sheep, Goats and Pigs. Figures in the parenthesis are percentages to total meat production.

Source: 1. Report on sample survey for estimation of production of milk, egg, wool and meat from 1978-79 to 1995-96, Directorate of Animal Husbandry and Veterinary Services, Government of Karnataka.

2. Taken from the official records of the Department of Animal Husbandry and Veterinary Services, Government of Karnataka, Bangalore.

Table 3.2

Share of Agriculture and Livestock Output to Gross Domestic Product (GDP)

		Share of Agriculture to GDP at factor cost*	*Share of Livestock** to GDP*	*Share of Livestock output (Gross)*** to Gross output from Agriculture*
			Percent	
1970-71	India	45.7	2.8	15.4
	Karnataka	48.4	0.9	9.9
1975-76	India	40.1	4.4	18.0
	Karnataka	43.0	2.9	12.1
1980-81	India	34.7	2.0	18.6
	Karnataka	39.1	2.1	11.1
1985-86	India	29.9	4.7	24.0
	Karnataka	32.2	4.7	21.2
1986-87	India	28.6	4.9	25.0
	Karnataka	34.0	4.7	19.9
1996-97	India	24.4	n.a	n.a
	Karnataka	30.0	7.9	26.6

Note: * Agriculture include livestock and sericulture.

** Value of livestock output minus fed of livestock.

*** For Karnataka, gross value of output from livestock does not include value of output from sericulture, whereas it is included at the all India level. Gross value of output from agriculture include value of output from livestock and sericulture, both for Karnataka as well as at the all India level.

Source: 1. National Accounts Statistics, 1983, 1989 and 1997, Central Statistical Organisation, Ministry of Planning, Government of India.

(*Contd.*)

2. Estimates of State Domestic Product, 1985, 1987 and 1989, Central Statistical Organisation, Ministry of Planning, Government of India.
3. Directorate of Economics and Statistics, Government of Karnataka, Bangalore.
4. State Domestic Product Karnataka- 1980-81 and 1990-91 to 1997-98, Directorate of Economics and Statistics, Bangalore, 1999.

In India the demand for sheep and goats as meat animals will increase further. With the increase in household income, the proportion of expenditure incurred on consumption of meat also increases. For the urban households with the increase in total expenditure, a decline in the proportion of amount spent on cereal and cereal substitutes and for milk and milk products was noticed in a majority of the states in the country, whereas the proportion of expenditure incurred on consumption of eggs, meat and fish increased or remained constant (Sinha and Giri, 1989). In Karnataka also the proportion of expenditure on cereal and cereal substitutes between 1977-78 to 1983 has declined both in urban and rural areas. Expenditure on milk and milk products has remained constant in rural areas but declined in urban centers. In rural areas expenditure on egg, meat and fish has increased, whereas in urban areas it remained constant (see Table 3.3). Further, Table 3.4 shows that according to the NSS reports, between the 32nd and 38th rounds, the per capita monthly expenditure on cereals, milk and milk products and egg, meat and fish has increased both in urban and rural areas, whereas the proportion of monthly per capita expenditure declined for cereals in rural areas. It remained constant in the case of milk and milk products but increased for egg, meat and fish. In urban areas the proportions declined for cereals and milk and milk products and remained constant for egg, meat and fish (Table 3.4). This shows that in India since there is a taboo as far as beef is concerned and not many like to have buffaloe meat in their food, meat of chicken, mutton and goat take their place in non-vegetarian diets. Unfortunately, a separate break-up for goat and sheep meat is not available.

Table 3.3
Changes in the Proportion of Expenditure During 1977-78 and January to December 1983

Commodities		*Increased*	*Decreased*	*Remained almost constant*
Cereal and Cereal Substitutes	Rural	-	√	-
	Urban	-	√	-
Milk and Milk products	Rural	-	-	√
	Urban	-	√	-
Egg, meat and fish	Rural	√	-	-
	Urban	-	-	√

Source : Sinha P and A. K. Giri, "Consumption of Livestock Products–Analysis and Comparison of Data of NSS 32nd and 38th Rounds", in *Livestock Economy of India,* Indian Society of Agricultural Economics, Oxford and IBH, New Delhi, 1989, (pp. 159-160).

Table 3.4
Per Capita Monthly Expenditure and their Proportions for Different Commodities in Karnataka: NSS 32nd and 38th Rounds

Commodity	*Rural*		*Urban*	
	32nd	*38th*	*32nd*	*38th*
Cereal and Cereal Substitutes (Rs.)	21.7	35.1	21.4	33.4
Percentage	33	30	24	20
Milk and Milk products (Rs.)	3.2	6.0	6.7	11.7
Percentage	5	5	8	7
Egg, meat and fish (Rs.)	1.6	3.5	2.5	5.6
Percentage	2	3	3	3

Source : As in Table 3.3.

Small ruminants contribute notably to the income and employment of rural population. Agriculture in India is largely based on mixed farming. The inherent nature of complementarities and supplementarities between crop cultivation and animal husbandry, made the farmers to keep small ruminants along with crop cultivation. Through stubble grazing, sheep and goats meet their fodder requirements at least for about 2 to 3 months in a year. The manure from small ruminants enriches the arable land as well as bring down the cost of cultivation. Farmers meet the immediate cash expenses on household consumption or on crop cultivation through the sale of one or two sheep and goats. Household members, the opportunity cost of whose labour is low/zero, depend on sheep and goats rearing both as main as well as subsidiary occupation. Common and other uncultivated public lands have helped the rural households particularly, the landless, to keep some of sheep and goats. With their unique qualities like adaptability to diverse conditions, less requirement of fodder and water, low level of capital requirement and surviving on dry grass, herbages, thorns and bushes from common property resources (CPRs), sheep and goats have become more suitable to farmers, particularly to the small and marginal farmers and landless households.

Concentration of sheep and goats is more in arid and semi-arid areas where irrigation potential is very low or nil. But after a certain period even in irrigated areas, when agricultural development reaches its plateau, farmers again concentrate on sheep and goats to increase their total income by using the crop residues. During this stage, the method of breeding is sedentary/stall feeding and with improved breeds of sheep and goats (India, Government of, 1987).

India has 15 well known breeds of goats, *viz.* Jamnapari, Surti, Beetal, Marwari, Barbari, Deccan, Malabari, Black Bengal, White Bengal, Gaddi, Kashmiri, Chegu, Mehsana, Sirohi and Osmanabadi. In Karnataka no specific breeds of goats have been mentioned. It could be described as 'desi' or local breeds. Broadly two kinds of goats are found in Karnataka—the long-legged or *meke,* and the short-legged or *kanchi meke.* The important sheep breeds of India are; Chanthang, Gurez, Karnah, Bhakarwal, Biangir, Bhadarwah or Gaddi, Bikaneri, Kathiawari, Deccani, Bellary, Hassan,

Mandya (Bannur/Bandur), Nellore, Jalauni, Muzaffarnagri, Madras red, Mecheri, Vembur, Keezhakaraisal, Ramnad white, Nilgiri and Coimbatore white. Karnataka has five important breeds of sheep; *i.e.* Deccani, Bellary, Hassan, Mandya and Nellore. Mandya breed is famous world over as one of the good mutton breeds. Bellary breed of sheep contribute black coarse wool which is much in demand for making carpets and coarse blankets known as Kamblis both within Karnataka as well as outside the state. It has been recorded that in the past a particular caste of people maintained a particular breed of sheep in Karnataka and only three breeds were identified. The *Gollar* breed maintained by the gollas (shepherds), the *Kurubar* breed maintained by the kurubas (shepherds) and the *yelaga* which is the rarest and maintained by both gollas and kurubas (Rice, 1897). White, brown and black colours are found in all the three breeds. The Kurubar is a small sheep, its flesh and wool are superior to those of the other two varieties. The gollar yield coarser wool. The yelaga which is rare and resembles a goat in the structure of the body and limbs. This breed is never shorn for their wool, being too coarse and this sheep shed their coats once a year. The kurubar and gollar sheep are shorn twice a year. The wool is all coarse and used in the manufacturing of rough blankets.

3.2 Trends in the Population of Small Ruminants and Their Spatial Distribution

To understand the trend and growth of ruminant population both in India and for Karnataka in different regions, data on total population of cattle, buffaloes, sheep and goats have been collected from different livestock census reports. As ruminant livestock depend to a larger extent on uncultivated public lands, forests and other common property resources (CPRs) for their fodder requirement, data on land utilisation also have been collected and analysed from different reports. Table 3.5 shows the position and growth of small and large ruminants in Karnataka and also in the country as a whole. Numerically, cattle dominate livestock; small ruminants formed 37.7 per cent of total ruminant livestock in Karnataka during 1990, and practically the same proportion—about 37 per cent—in the country as a whole during 1992. In Karnataka sheep population increased by 15 per cent between 1956 to 1990, as against 30 per cent in the country as a whole. Goat population has increased more than cattle and sheep both in Karnataka and in India. It has increased by 50 per cent in Karnataka and by 108 per cent in India during the same period. The lower growth rate of sheep both in Karnataka and India as compared with goats and buffaloes is probably due to the higher rate of consumption of sheep than of the other ruminants. It may also be due to increased mortality among sheep, which may again due to the non-availability of good fodder. As the quantity and quality of common property resources including grazing lands has declined, sheep have to graze intensively on whatever available herbages, and hence are vulnerable to many diseases. Sheep are less prolific and need good quality pastures, unlike goats which survive much longer on the herbages from degraded hill slopes, forests and barren lands. Goats and cattle manage to get good fodder through extensive grazing. Cattle and buffaloes are fed on crop residues also. Though goats have also been slaughtered on a large scale, we find remarkable increase in their population, which is due to their high prolificacy and high resistance to adverse conditions. Goats are more hardy and less susceptible to disease. During adverse conditions like drought, goats withstand the stress and after the disaster the herd grows much more rapidly than other ruminants.

A major problem affecting small ruminants is that lands which are a source of fodder for them are declining in quantity as also quality. Small ruminants are maintained on uncultivated lands, forests and other CPRs. Though stubble grazing meets some of the fodder requirements of these animals, its role has declined after the Green Revolution. Due to technological change involving short duration crops, and also attraction of commercial crops, farmers are cultivating double and annual crops, by which both the share of residues to grain and the period for stubble grazing has gone down in several areas. Barren and uncultivated waste lands, pastures

Table 3.5

Ruminant Population (India and Karnataka) (Population in Lakhs)

Year	Cattle		Buffaloes		Sheep		Goats		Total Ruminants	
	India	*Karnataka*	*India*	*Karnataka*	*India*	*Karnataka*	*India*	*Karnataka*	*India*	*Karnataka*
1956	1587	90	449	27	392	41	555	26	2983	182
	(100)	(100)	(100)	(100)	(100)	(100)	(100)	(100)	(100)	(100)
1961	1756	97	512	30	402	48	609	29	3279	204
	(111)	(108)	(114)	(111)	(103)	(117)	(110)	(112)	(110)	(111)
1966	1762	97	530	29	420	47	646	28	3358	201
	(111)	(108)	(118)	(107)	(107)	(115)	(116)	(108)	(113)	(109)
1972	1783	100	574	32	400	47	675	37	3432	216
	(112)	(111)	(128)	(119)	(102)	(115)	(122)	(142)	(115)	(117)
1977	1801	102	620	33	409	45	756	34	3586	214
	(113)	(113)	(138)	(122)	(104)	(110)	(136)	(131)	(120)	(116)
1983	1908	113	690	36	481	48	952	45	4031	242
	(120)	(126)	(154)	(133)	(123)	(117)	(172)	(173)	(135)	(132)
1999	2046	102	842	40	508	47	1153	39	4549	228
	(129)	(113)	(188)	(148)	(130)	(115)	(208)	(150)	(152)	(124)

(Contd.)

Note : Total Ruminants include cattle, buffaloes, sheep and goats.

* For Karnataka the latest Census available is for the year 1990, whereas at the all India level it is for 1992.

Source:

1. 13th and 14th Quinquennial livestock census 1983 and 1990, the Department of Animal Husbandry and veterinary services, Government of Karnataka, Bangalore.
2. Indian Livestock Census, Vol. II, 1o56, 1966, 1972, 1987 and 1992, Directorate of Economics and Statistics, Ministry of Agriculture, Government of India, New Delhi.
3. Indian Agriculture in Brief, 20th edition, Directorate of Economics and Statistics, Government of India, 1985.
4. Agricultural Situation in India, October, 1983 to November, 1986.
5. Pandeya, S.C., 'Status of Indian Rangelands', Presidential Address, 3rd International Rangeland Congress, November, 1988, New Delhi.

and forests are the major source of fodder to the ruminants in Karnataka. While the ruminant population has increased by 24 per cent from 1956 to 1990 in Karnataka, grazing lands such a cultivable and uncultivable waste lands and pastures have decreased by 29.7 per cent during the same period. At the all India level ruminant population has increased by 52 per cent from 1956 to 1992, whereas barren, cultivable and uncultivable waste lands, pastures and other grazing lands have decreased by 30.5 per cent during 1955-56 to 1991-92. It is not likely that this decline in grazing lands has been compensated by an increase in their productivity. Though the area under forest has increased both in Karnataka and in India, it may not support the increasing ruminant population due to its own degradation. Also, the environmental awareness about the forests has led to its strict conservation and banning of grazing by small ruminants in several areas. On the other hand the net area sown has increased in Karnataka by 7.1 per cent during 56-57 to 89-90. At the all India level, net area sown has increased more than in Karnataka (39 per cent) during 1955-56 to 1991-92 (see Table 3.6). As a result of which both the livestock sector and the resource base are under greater stress. The quality of ruminants in terms of productivity is fast declining. On the other hand the carrying capacity of rangelands has also decreased. The unregulated and continued pressure of grazing on these lands has led to its further degradation and hence one of the major causes of ecological imbalance. Problems like droughts, floods, soil erosion, siltation etc. are due to the bad health of these rangelands. Table 3.7 shows that the pressure of grazing by ruminant livestock has increased both at the all India level as well as in Karnataka over the period 1956-57 to 1991-92. A larger number of ruminants have to be fed per hectare of pasture and other grazing lands now than during 1956-57. Further, pressure on the grazing lands by the large ruminants is much more than the small ruminants both in Karnataka and in India. One hectare of pasture and other grazing land had to feed 1.6 animal units of sheep and goats during 1989-90 as compared with 12.9 animal units of cattle and buffaloes in Karnataka. It was

Table 3.6

Land Utilisation (thousand hectares) (Karnataka and India)

Year	Total Geographical Area	Forests	Barren & uncultivable waste	Cultivable waste	Permanent Pastures and other grazing lands	Land under miscellaneous tree crops and grovers	Other fallows	Net area Shown	Net irrigated area
1	2	3	4	5	6	7	8	9	10
Karnataka									
1956-57	19065	2671	904	651	1781	388	473	9999	735
		(14.0)	(4.7)	(3.4)	(9.3)	(2.0)	(2.5)	(52.4)	(3.9)
1960-61	19044	2688	895	651	1726	364	509	10110	790
		(14.1)	(4.7)	(3.4)	(9.1)	(1.9)	(2.7)	(53.1)	(4.1)
1966-67	19310	2701	916	650	1653	364	676	10014	1022
		(14.0)	(4.7)	(3.4)	(8.6)	(1.9)	(3.5)	(51.9)	(5.3)
1970-71	19135	2890	839	615	1619	311	672	10248	1366
		(15.1)	(4.4)	(3.2)	(8.5)	(1.6)	(3.5)	(53.6)	(7.1)
1976-77	19064	2914	874	559	1499	330	–	9206	1215
		(15.3)	(4.6)	(2.9)	(7.9)	(1.7)	NA	(48.3)	(6.4)

(Contd.)

(Contd.)

1	2	3	4	5	6	7	8	9	10
1982-83	19050	3029	829	495	1260	332	490	10356	1486
		(15.8)	(4.3)	(2.6)	6.6)	(1.7)	(2.6)	(54.0)	(7.7)
1989-90	19050	3074	799	447	1100	317	403	10708	2094
		(16.1)	(4.2)	(2.3)	(5.8)	(1.7)	(2.1)	(56.2)	(11.0)
India									
1955-56	328726	51343	34476	21537	11473	5885	12544	129156	22758
		(15.6)	(10.5)	(6.6)	(3.5)	(1.8)	(3.8)	(39.3)	(6.9)
1960-61	328726	54052	35911	19212	13966	4459	11180	131199	24661
		(16.4)	(10.9)	(5.8)	(4.2)	(1.4)	(3.4)	(40.5)	(7.5)
1965-66	328726	61543	34327	16965	14810	4076	9262	136198	26344
		(18.7)	(10.4)	(5.2)	(4.5)	(1.2)	(2.8)	(41.4)	(8.0)
1970-71	328726	63917	28161	17500	13262	4298	8759	140784	31103
		(19.4)	(8.6)	(5.3)	(4.0)	(1.3)	(2.7)	(42.8)	(9.5)
1976-77	328726	67163	22129	17149	12529	3976	9696	140183	35147
		(20.4)	(6.7)	(5.2)	(3.8)	(1.2)	(2.9)	(42.6)	(10.7)

(Contd.)

(Contd.)

1	*2*	*3*	*4*	*5*	*6*	*7*	*8*	*9*	*10*
1982-83	328726	67161	20139	16313	11956	3554	9503	141769	39969
		(20.4)	(6.1)	(5.0)	(3.6)	(1.1)	(2.9)	(43.1)	(12.2)
1984-85	328726	67157	20068	15738	11934	3385	9552	140715	41779
		(20.40)	(6.1)	(4.8)	(3.6)	(1.0)	(2.9)	(42.8)	(12.7)
1991-92	328726	67763	19394	15001	11299	3754	9946	179979	n.a.
		(20.6)	(5.9)	(4.6)	(3.4)	(1.1)	(3.0)	(54.8)	

Note: Figures in the parenthesis are percentages to total geographical area.
NA = Not available.

Source: 1. Agricultural situation in India, July 1985.

2. Annual season and crop Report, 1956-57, 1960-61 and 1966-67.
3. Indian Agricultural Statistics, Vol. II, 1974-75 to 1976-77, Directorate of Economics and Statistics, Ministry of Agriculture, New Delhi.
4. Indian Agriculture in Brief, 7th, 17th, 19th, 20th, 21st, 22nd and 24th Editions, Directorate of Economics and Statistics, Department of Agriculture and Co-operation, Government of India, New Delhi.
5. Directorate of Economics and Statistics, Government of Karnataka, Bangalore.

Table 3.7

Animal Units Per Hectare of Different Types of Land in Karnataka and India

Year	*Small Ruminants per hectare of pastures and other grazing lands*	*Small Ruminants per hectare of Barren, Cultivable, unculti-vable and other fallow lands*	*Small Ruminants per hectare of forest*	*Large Ruminants per hectare of pastures and other grazing lands*	*Large Ruminants per hectare of Barren, Cultivable, uncultivable and other fallow lands*	*Large Ruminants per hectare of forest*	*Small Ruminants per hectare of 2, 3, and 4*	*Large Ruminants per hectare of 5, 6 & 7*
(1)	(2)	(3)	(4)	(5)	(6)	(7)	(8)	(9)
Karnataka								
1956-57	0.7	0.7	0.5	6.5	5.7	4.4	0.2	1.8
1960-61	0.9	0.7	0.6	7.4	6.2	4.7	0.2	2.0
1966-67	0.9	0.7	0.6	7.6	5.6	4.7	0.2	1.9
1970-71	1.0	0.8	0.6	8.2	6.2	4.6	0.3	2.0
1976-77	1.1	0.8	0.5	9.0	6.6	4.6	0.2	2.1

(Contd.)

(Contd.)

(1)	*(2)*	*(3)*	*(4)*	*(5)*	*(6)*	*(7)*	*(8)*	*(9)*
1982-83	1.5	1.0	0.6	11.9	8.2	4.9	0.3	2.4
1989-90	1.6	1.0	0.6	12.9	8.6	4.6	0.3	2.4
India								
1955-56	1.7	0.3	0.4	17.7	3.0	4.0	0.1	1.5
1960-61	1.4	0.3	0.4	16.2	3.4	4.2	0.2	1.7
1965-66	1.4	0.4	0.3	15.5	3.8	3.7	0.2	1.7
1970-71	1.6	0.4	0.3	17.8	4.3	3.7	0.2	1.8
1976-77	1.9	0.5	0.3	19.3	4.9	3.6	0.2	1.9
1982-83	2.4	0.6	0.4	21.7	5.7	3.9	0.2	2.1
1987-88	2.7	0.7	0.5	22.6	5.9	4.0	0.3	2.2
1991-92	2.9	0.7	0.5	25.5	6.5	4.2	0.3	2.3

Note : One Animal Unit = One Cow / Buffalo / Bullock, 2 Cow and Buffalo Calves, 5 Sheep/Goats (equivalence adopted from Jodha, 1986)

much more at 2.9 and 25.5 animal units respectively for small and large ruminants at the country as a whole. This can be compared with optimal carrying capacity of grazing lands in India estimated at about one cow per 2.4-4 hectares and 2.5 sheep per hectare (Chakravarty, 1971 as quoted in Pandeya, 1988, p. 13).

Table 3.8 shows that in Karnataka the share of sheep and goats to total ruminant livestock is higher in droughtprone districts than the non-droughtprone and mixed type of districts. Large ruminants, on the other hand dominate in the non-droughtprone districts. This is understandable because the poorer fodder base in droughtprone districts is relatively more suitable to support small ruminants requiring less fodder than large ruminants. Even the growth of sheep and goats is much higher in droughtprone districts than the other districts. Sheep and goats constitute more than 44 per cent of total ruminants in the droughtprone districts during 1990, whereas cattle dominate in the non-droughtprone districts by 65 per cent of total ruminants during the same year.

Paradoxically, the proportion of net sown area is higher in droughtprone districts (62.6 per cent in 1989-90) than in non-droughtprone districts (31.7 per cent in 1989-90). This is suggestive of efforts to compensate for lower productivity of land by extending the margin of cultivation. Also, the non-droughtprone districts have more forests. The lands which afford grazing by ruminants, namely, forests, cultivable and uncultivable wastes, permanent pastures and other grazing lands, are relatively more in non-droughtprone districts (53.9 per cent in 1989-90) than in droughtprone districts (23.3 per cent in 1989-90). (see Table 3.9). The point we would like to highlight here is that, though sheep and goats are playing a very important role in the droughtprone districts, the fodder base for these animals is much less and continuously shrinking.

The problem is much more serious if we look at the extent of pressure of different types of ruminant livestock in Karnataka across different types of districts. Though the concentration of large ruminants is more in non-droughtprone

Table 3.8

Ruminant Population (in lakhs) in Karnataka According to Type of Districts

Districts	No. of Districts	Cattle					Buffaloes				
		1956	1966	1977	1983	1990	1956	1966	1977	1983	1990
1	2	3	4	5	6	7	8	9	10	11	12
DPD	9	49 (45.0)	51 (44.0)	53 (43.8)	61 (3.0)	55 (41.3)	13 (11.9)	13 (11.2)	15 (12.4)	16 (11.3)	19 (14.3)
NDPD	6	22 (68.8)	25 (69.4)	27 (67.5)	28 (66.7)	26 (65.0)	6 (18.6)	7 (19.4)	8 (20.0)	8 (19.0)	9 (22.5)
Mixed	4	19 (44.2)	21 (42.9)	22 (41.5)	24 (41.4)	21 (37.5)	8 (18.6)	9 (18.4)	10 (18.9)	12 (20.7)	13 (23.2)
State	19	90 (48.9)	97 (28.3)	102 (47.7)	113 (46.7)	102 (44.5)	27 (14.7)	29 (14.4)	33 (15.3)	36 (14.9)	41 (17.9)

(Contd.)

(Contd.)

Sheep					Goats				
1956	*1966*	*1977*	*1983*	*1990*	*1956*	*1966*	*1977*	*1983*	*1990*
13	*14*	*15*	*16*	*17*	*18*	*19*	*20*	*21*	*22*
29	33	31	34	34	18	19	22	31	25
(26.6)	(28.6)	(25.6)	(23.9)	(25.6)	(16.5)	(16.4)	(18.2)	(21.8)	(18.8)
2	2	2	2	2	2	3	3	4	3
(6.3)	(5.6)	(5.0)	(4.8)	(5.0)	(6.3)	(5.6)	(7.5)	(9.5)	(7.5)
10	12	12	12	12	6	7	9	10	10
(23.3)	(24.5)	(22.6)	(20.7)	(21.4)	(14.0)	(14.3)	(17.9)	(17.2)	(17.9)
41	47	45	48	48	26	28	34	45	38
(22.3)	(23.4)	(21.0)	(19.8)	(21.0)	(14.1)	(13.9)	(15.9)	(18.6)	(16.0)

Note: DPD = Drought Prone Districts; NDPD = Non-Drought Prone Districts; Mixed = Mixed type of Districts. Figures in the parenthesis are percentages to total ruminants.

Source: 1. 13th and 14th Quinquennial Livestock Census, 1983 and 1990, Department of Animal Husbandry and Veterinary Services, Government of Karnataka, Bangalore.

2. Indian Livestock Census, Vol. II, 1956 and 1966, Directorate of Economics and Statistics, Government of India.

3. Statistical Abstract of Karnataka, 1978-79, Bureau of Economics and Statistics, Government of Karnataka, Bangalore.

Table 3.9

Percentage Distribution of Land Utilisation in Karnataka Across Different Types of Districts

Year	*Regions*	*Total Geographical area (1000 hectares)*	*Forests*	*Barren, cultivable, uncultivable waste and other fallow land*	*Permanent pastures and other grazing lands*	*Other types of land*	*Total Net Sown Area*
1	*2*	*3*	*4*	*5*	*6*	*7*	*8*
1956-57	DPD	100 (10653)	8.1	9.5	8.8	14.0	59.6
"	NDPD	100 (4542)	32.4	13.4	12.5	16.2	25.5
"	Mixed	100 (3870)	8.8	10.4	7.2	9.3	64.3
"	State	100 (19065)	14.0 (2671)	10.6 (2028)	9.3 (1781)	13.6 (2586)	52.4 (9999)
1966-67	DPD	100 (10718)	8.1	11.4	8.7	14.5	57.1
"	NDPD	100 (4581)	33.0	14.2	10.3	14.2	28.3

(Contd.)

(Contd.)

1	*2*	*3*	*4*	*5*	*6*	*7*	*8*
1966-67	Mixed	100 (4013)	7.9	9.0	6.2	12.3	64.6
"	State	100 (19310)	14.0 (2701)	11.6 (2242)	8.6 (1653)	14.0 (2700)	51.9 (10014)
1976-77	DPD	100 (10581)	8.7	10.6	7.8	20.7	52.3
"	NDPD	100 (4582)	35.4	13.2	10.7	13.6	27.1
"	Mixed	100 (3901)	35.4	13.2	10.7	13.6	27.1
"	State	100 (19064)	15.3 (2914)	10.8 (2050)	7.6 (1449)	18.0 (3445)	48.3 (9206)
1982-83	DPD	100 (10576)	8.8	9.5	6.4	15.0	60.3
"	NDPD	100 (4589)	37.3	11.3	9.1	12.2	30.1

(Contd.)

(Contd.)

1	2	3	4	5	6	7	8
1982-83	Mixed	100 (3885)	9.8	7.5	4.1	11.5	67.1
"	State	100 (19050)	15.9	9.5	6.6	13.6	54.5
1989-90	DPD	100 (10576)	8.9	8.8	5.6	14.1	62.6
"	NDPD	100 (4590)	38.0	10.0	5.9	12.2	31.7
"	Mixed	100 (3883)	9.9	6.8	3.5	18.0	67.8
"	State	100 (19050)	16.1 (3074)	8.7 (1649)	5.8 (1100)	13.2 (2518)	56.2 (10708)

Note: Figures in the parenthesis are absolute figures in thousand hectares.
DPD = Drought Prone Districts; NDPD = Non-Drought Prone Districts; Mixed = Mixed type of Districts.

Source:
1. Agriculture situation in India, July 1985.
2. Annual season and crop report 1956-57 and 1966-67.
3. Indian Agricultural Statistics, Vol. II, 1974-75 to 1976-77, Directorate of Economics and Statistics, Ministry of Agriculture, New Delhi.
4. Directorate of Economics and Statistics, Govt. of Karnataka, Bangalore, 1991.

Table 3.10

Animal Units Per Hectare of Different Types of Land in Karnataka Across Different Types of Districts

Year	Small Ruminants per hectare of pastures and other grazing lands	Small Ruminants per hectare of Barren, Cultivable uncultivable and other fallow lands	Small Ruminants per hectare of forest	Large Ruminants per hectare of pastures and other lands	Large Ruminants per hectare of Barren, Cultivable, grazing and other fallow lands	Large Ruminants per hectare of forest uncultivable	Small Ruminants per hectare of 2, 3, and 4	Large Ruminants per hectare of 5, 6 & 7
(1)	(2)	(3)	(4)	(5)	(6)	(7)	(8)	(9)
DPD								
1956	1.00	0.93	1.09	6.63	6.11	7.22	0.34	2.21
1966	1.12	0.85	1.20	7.01	5.31	7.51	0.34	2.16
1977	1.28	0.94	1.14	8.32	6.12	7.46	0.37	2.39
1983	1.92	1.30	1.39	11.43	7.74	8.32	0.50	2.97
1990	2.02	1.28	1.25	12.51	7.92	7.76	0.48	2.99

(Contd.)

(Contd.)

(1)	(2)	(3)	(4)	(5)	(6)	(7)	(8)	(9)
NDPD								
1956	0.13	0.12	0.05	0.83	4.48	1.86	0.03	1.03
1966	0.17	0.12	0.05	6.67	4.84	2.08	0.03	1.19
1977	0.19	0.15	0.06	6.93	5.62	2.10	0.03	1.25
1983	0.26	0.21	0.06	8.62	6.94	2.11	0.04	1.36
1990	0.25	0.21	0.05	9.23	7.58	1.99	0.04	1.35
Mixed								
1956	1.12	0.78	0.91	9.69	6.72	7.90	0.31	2.64
1966	1.53	1.05	1.19	11.84	8.14	9.24	0.41	3.17
1977	2.38	1.35	1.18	17.58	9.98	8.72	0.50	3.68
1983	2.84	1.58	1.20	22.17	12.31	9.34	0.51	4.28
1990	3.25	1.69	1.16	24.76	12.90	8.85	0.57	4.33

(Contd.)

(Contd.)

(1)	(2)	(3)	(4)	(5)	(6)	(7)	(8)	(9)
State								
1956	0.75	0.66	0.50	6.53	5.74	4.36	0.21	1.80
1966	0.91	0.7	0.56	7.64	5.63	4.68	0.23	1.92
1977	1.09	0.77	0.54	9.32	6.59	4.63	0.25	2.11
1983	1.48	1.03	0.62	11.86	8.24	4.94	0.31	2.45
1990	1.57	1.04	0.56	12.92	8.62	4.62	0.30	2.44

Note : One Animal Unit = One Cow / Buffalo / Bullock, 2 Cow and Buffalo Calves, 5 Sheep / Goats (equivalence adopted from Jodha, 1986).

DPD = Drought Prone Districts; NDPD = Non-Drought Prone Districts; Mixed = Mixed type of Districts.

districts (as we have mentioned earlier), Table 3.10 below shows that the pressure on rangelands by large ruminants is much more in droughtprone and mixed types of districts than in the non-droughtprone districts. During 1990 one hectare of pasture, barren, cultivable and uncultivable lands, forest and other fallow land had to feed 2.99 and 4.33 animal units of large ruminants in droughtprone and mixed type of districts, respectively. This is higher in comparison with non-droughtprone districts, where only 1.35 animal units of large ruminants are fed per hectare of such lands. Further, in droughtprone districts, though the relative concentration of small ruminants is more than the large ruminants, the pressure on range lands by these animals is much less. Only 0.48 animal unit of small ruminants per hectare of pasture, cultivable, uncultivable, barren, forests and other fallow lands, are fed in these districts during the same period, compared to 3 animal units of large ruminants. This shows that in droughtprone districts, the danger of further degradation of rangelands through grazing pressure is seen more from large ruminants than from sheep and goats.

4

PROFILE OF THE STUDY AREA

4.1 Geographical, Historical and Infrastructural Background of the Study Area (Kolar District, Bagepalli Taluk and the Selected Villages)

Kolar is the eastern most district of Karnataka State. It belongs to the Southern Maidan (plains) group of districts as distinct from the mountainous western portions of the state called Malnad. It is situated between 12° 46′ and 13° 58′ north latitude and 77° 21′ and 78° 35′ east longitude. Total geographical area of the district is 8223 sq. kms. with a length of about 135 kms from north to south and about 135 kms from east to west. It is bounded by Bangalore and Tumkur districts of Karnataka on the West and on all other sides surrounded by the adjoining districts of Andhra Pradesh and Tamil Nadu States. It formed a part of the old princely state of Mysore before the States' Reorganisation.

In area Kolar occupies 12th place among the districts of Karnataka. The general plateau surface is interrupted by a number of hills and peaks of varying heights, particularly in the northern part of the district. Apart from the principal chain of hills which runs in the north, a line of low hills consisting of mere rising grounds or mounds passes in the district. Minerals, rivers, forests and cultivable lands are the main natural resources. Forests are very meagre. Area under forest is barely 10 per cent of the total geographical area of the district, as compared with National Standard of 33 per cent. In hilly tracts where soils are rocky, gravelly or very shallow, forests are in a very poor condition. Vegetation in these areas is either of dry deciduous type or of thorny scrub type. Due to over use for firewood and charcoal, forests in Kolar district are in a very bad condition.

The rivers and streams of the district are small and seasonal, which remain mostly dry due to scanty rainfall. On an average there are only 47 rainy days in a year. This also varies from 43 in Bagepalli taluka to 54 in Chikballapur taluka and 64 at Nandi hills. The central and eastern parts of the district forming the palar valley are undulating and well cultivated.

As per 1991 census, the share of Kolar district's population to the state population was 4.9 per cent. Within the district rural population constitute 76.7 per cent. Density of population per sq.km. in the district was 284 which was much higher than that at the state level, (being 235 persons per sq.km. in the state). Per capita availability of land with reference to total geographical area and the 1991 population was 0.35 hectares. If net cultivated area is taken into consideration, the per capita availability of land moves further down to 0.17 hectares. Further, there are many marginal and small farmers in the district.

There exist thousands of ancient irrigation tanks which occupy an important place in the prosperity and development of the district. The soils on the high grounds are red and gravelly. In the valleys one can find loamy and good soils. Red and dark soils are found in the eastern parts of the district. Agriculture is largely based on dry farming. Ragi is the major food crop. Apart from ragi, sugarcane, paddy, groundnut and mulberry are also grown. Silk worm rearing is one of the important activities of the rural people. Productivity of food crops is very low. The estimated yield rate per hectare of paddy and ragi during 1980-81 was 1280 kg and 820 kg respectively.

Mostly ragi, jowar, pulses and millets are grown in dry land. Wet land is used for the cultivation of sugarcane, mulberry, tobacco, paddy and vegetables. Coconut, citrus fruits, mangoes and grapes are grown on garden land.

Animal husbandry in the district is complementary to agriculture. Organic manure is still the chief fertilizer. The development of agriculture depends to a greater extent on available livestock which are the main source of organic manure. Keeping a pair of bullocks, a few non-descript cows or buffaloes is essential for any farmer. The social status of a cultivator is judged by the number of cattle he owns. Draught power is an essential component in the farming system. Sheep and goats are also playing a very important role in the district's rural economy. All classes of rural households, particularly a large number of small and marginal farmers and landless households keep sheep and goats as a subsidiary but a significant source of income.

Kolar like other districts in the state is subject to variations in seasons. March to May constitute the hot season. The South-West monsoon season last from June to October. May is generally the hottest month with a mean daily temperature of 34.2°C at K. G. F. Maximum temperature sometimes go upto 40°C. The average annual rainfall is 730.5 mm, and the precipitation during the South-West monsoon constitutes 69 per cent of the total annual rainfall. This district is known for its frequent suffering due to vagaries of monsoon resulting in famine and droughts. In the closing years of 18th century the district suffered from a dreadful famine. When Lord Cornwallis invaded the district, many died of starvation. Between 1851 and 1861 year after year the people of the district witnessed misery and scarcity conditions. The great famine of 1875-76 and 1876-77 proved most calamitous in the history of Kolar district. In the present century, 1908-09 and 1923 were affected by severe famines. There are no reports of such severe famines in subsequent years, but the district has been subject to periodical sufferings from scanty rains and droughts (Census of India, 1981).

Industrially Kolar district may be considered as well developed. This is particularly welcome for a drought-prone district, since diversification of the economy is an effective way of dealing with droughtproneness. Factories like Bharat Gold Mines Ltd., Bharat Earth Movers Ltd., and Co-operative Sugar Factory are situated in the district. Small scale industries like engineering, automobiles, steel furniture, agricultural implements, tiles, bricks, slate pencils, wooden furnitures and saw mills are also found. Silk reeling and handloom weaving are the other important cottage industries. About 10,000 handlooms are there in the district. Coarse woollen blankets called 'Kolar Kamblis' are prepared on about 1000 Kambli-weaving looms in the district. 'Kolar Kamblis' are much in demand by the local farmers as well as by the farmers from neighbouring districts. Kolar district is famous for its gold production.

Bagepalli taluka is situated in the northern part of Kolar district bordering the State of Andhra Pradesh. Total geographical area of the taluk is 93039.81 hectares (930.40 sq.kms), and there are 208 inhabited villages. In total there are 228 villages in the taluk, out of which 20 villages are uninhabited. Average geographical area of an inhabited village is highest in Bagepalli taluka (436 hectares) as compared with the district average, being 288.7 hectares. Though in terms of area, Bagepalli taluk is the biggest, in population size it occupies the 10th place in the district, with the lowest density of 136 persons per sq.km. during 1981[7]. Even in the case of density

7. Since for Bagepalli taluka population data for 1991 is not available, we have taken the population as per 1981 census.

of rural population, it occupies the last place in the district (density being 128 in rural areas of Bagepalli taluk as compared with Kolar taluka, where the density is 227). This also shows that Bagepalli taluka is more droughtprone than the other talukas in Kolar district. The share of rural population to total population in the taluk constitute 93.8 per cent during the same year.

Many families in the villages of Bagepalli taluka depend on subsistence agriculture with animal husbandry. Though modern technology has been introduced in agriculture, most of the farmers are not able to adopt it due to their limited resources. Resource base of the region like soil fertility, rainfall, vegetation etc. is also poor. A large number of farmers still depend on only one rainfed kharif crop annually. Though the percentage of net cultivated area to total area is high (70 per cent) in the taluka, the proportion of net irrigated area to total net cultivated area is very less, being 10.7 per cent, as compared with the district where it is 14.36 per cent. Source of irrigation is mainly the traditional tanks, which are fully dependent on regular rainfall. There are a few dug wells also, but their share of irrigation is marginal and confined to the rich farmers. Introducing irrigation in all the areas is also not possible due to the geographical conditions and the high cost of tapping ground water which is also uncertain and limited only to the village elites.

A substantial proportion of area under uncultivated lands (culturable waste, gauchar/gomals, groves and area not available for cultivation) are found in this taluka. Around 24.9 per cent of total geographical area can be categorised as uncultivated lands, which are largely used for grazing, fuelwood collection etc. by the rural households. Though some proportion of geographical area has been categorised as forests, but actually there is no proper forests found here. Only about 5.1 per cent of the total geographical area is under forest, merely with scrub and bush types of vegetation. As a whole in this region one can largely find areas with scrub and bush type of vegetation with hill slopes and gravelly lands, with harsh environment, which has enabled many rural households to keep a few sheep and goats permanently. Due to erratic and less rainfall, the gravelly soils have become less productive for crop cultivation. Animal husbandry, particularly sheep and goats rearing either as main or subsidiary source of income is a helpful proposition in the taluk for many households, particularly to the poor and landless.

4.2 Socio-Economic Profile of Households in the Selected Villages - Caste, Land Holdings, Family Size, Livestock, Occupation etc.

The selected villages-Achepalli, Neergantipalli and Gurraldinne constitute a cluster of three villages in Bagepalli taluk. Put together there are 285 households with different castes. More than 40 per cent of the total households belong to scheduled castes and scheduled tribes. This is higher than normal. The second largest social group belongs to the forward castes, which again includes a large proportion of Vokkaligas (a land owning caste). Though there are many caste groups in the study villages, the forward castes own a large proportion of cultivable lands. The largest group among the rich peasants are the forward castes (being 75.3 per cent) and there are only three landless households among these castes. On the other hand, though scheduled caste and scheduled tribe are numerically the major caste group in the villages, they are mostly poor and landless, except a few who have become rich peasants in recent years (see Table 4.1).

Table 4.1 also shows that among the rich peasants, a large number of forward caste households have taken up the rearing of small ruminants, as compared with the backward and scheduled caste and scheduled tribe households. On the other hand, among the landless families only scheduled caste and scheduled tribe (4 households) have taken up small ruminant rearing. This shows that rearing sheep and goats is entering largely into the hands of land owning households.

Table 4.1
Distribution of Total Households Across Class of Farmers and Across Different Castes in the Selected Village

Caste	Rich Peasants			Poor Peasants			Landless labour			All		
	HSR	HWSR	Total	HSR	HWSR	Total	HSR	HWSR	Total	HSR	HWSR	Total
1	*2*	*3*	*4*	*5*	*6*	*7*	*8*	*9*	*10*	*11*	*12*	*13*
Vokkaliga	27	26	53	12	19	31	-	-	-	39	45	84
	(73.0)	(59.1)	(65.4)	(19.7)	(17.1)	(18.0)				(38.2)	(24.6)	(29.5)
Balajiga	2	3	5	-	1	1	-	1	1	2	5	7
	(5.4)	(6.8)	(6.2)		(0.9)	(0.6)		(3.6)	(3.1)	(2.0)	(2.7)	(2.5)
Agasa	2	2	4	2	13	15	-	2	2	4	17	21
	(5.4)	(4.5)	(4.9)	(3.3)	(11.7)	(8.7)		(7.1)	(6.3)	(3.9)	(9.3)	(7.4)
Lambani	2	-	2	-	-	-	-	2	2	4	17	21
	(5.4)		(2.5)					(7.1)	(6.3)	(3.9)	(9.3)	(7.4)
Beda	2	-	2	-	-	-	-	2	2	2	2	4
	(5.4)		(2.5)					(7.1)	(6.3)	(2.0)	(1.1)	(1.4)
SC	2	7	9	34	53	87	4	12	16	40	72	112
	(5.4)	(15.9)	(11.1)	(55.7)	(47.7)	(50.6)	(100)	(42.9)	(50.0)	(39.2)	(39.3)	(39.3)
Myadru	-	-	-	1	2	3	-	-	-	1	2	3
				(1.6)	(1.8)	(1.7)				(1.0)	(1.1)	(1.1)
Bhovi	-	-	-	-	16	16	-	6	6	-	22	22
					(14.5)	(9.3)		(21.4)	(18.8)		(12.0)	(7.7)

(Contd.)

(Contd.)

1	*2*	*3*	*4*	*5*	*6*	*7*	*8*	*9*	*10*	*11*	*12*	*13*
Barber	-	2 (4.5)	2 (4.5)	-	2 (1.8)	2 (1.2)	-	2 (7.1)	2 (6.3)	-	6 (3.3)	6 (2.1)
Idiga	-	1 (2.3)	1 (1.2)	-	1 (0.9)	1 (0.6)	-	-	-	-	2 (1.1)	6 (2.1)
Vishwa-karma	-	1 (2.3)	1 (1.2)	-	2 (1.8)	2 (1.2)	-	1 (3.6)	1 (3.1)	-	4 (2.2)	4 (1.4)
Vysyas	-	1 (2.3)	1 (1.2)	-	1 (0.9)	1 (0.6)	-	-	-	-	2 (1.1)	2 (0.7)
Brahmin	-	1 (2.3)	1 (1.2)	-	-	-	-	1 (3.6)	1 (3.1)	-	2 (1.1)	2 (0.7)
Golla	-	-	-	-	1 (0.9)	1 (0.6)	-	-	-	-	1 (0.5)	1 (0.4)
Kuruba	-	-	-	-	-	-	-	1 (3.6)	1 (3.1)	-	1 (0.5)	1 (0.4)
Total	37 (100)	44 (100)	81 (100)	61 (100)	111 (100)	172 (100)	4 (100)	28 (100)	32 (100)	102 (100)	183 (100)	285 (100)

Note: Figures in the brackets are percentages to total households.
HSR = Households with small ruminants.
HWSR = Households without small ruminants.

It is no longer the *kuruba* or the *golla* castes (shepherds) alone which keeps small ruminants but other castes too. In fact Table 4.1 shows that in the study villages kuruba and golla families have not maintained these animals. On the other hand, many households which belong to the forward castes like the vokkaligas have maintained them. Our experience shows that in other parts of Karnataka many families which belong to the *lingayats*, an upper caste, are also maintaining goats and sheep. The traditional association of keeping goats and sheep almost exclusively with the backward castes is not any longer common. This does not necessarily mean that the condition of backward castes has become dismal. Thus, some of the sociological problems like a shepherd unmarried girl not getting a good bride groom is also not common. Marriage and education depend on the economic condition of the household. Many households have married their daughters, constructed new houses, educated some of their children out of the income from small ruminants.

Further, the other characteristics of the rural households can be seen from Table 5.2 below. Though the rich peasants constitute only 28.4 per cent of the total households in the sample villages, their command over other factors of production is substantial. The proportions of land, and of the large and small ruminants held by them constitute 68.9 percent, 55.4 per cent and 57.7 per cent respectively. Their average land holding size is 9.2 acres with average number of 7.3 persons per household, as compared with poor peasants who own on an average only 1.9 acres of land per household with an average family size of about five persons. Particularly in a droughtprone region, 1.9 acres of land per household is a non-viable holding. Even 9.2 acres of dry land per household is not a large holding.

Table 4.2

Average Size of Population, Land Holding Size and Ruminant Livestock Holding Across Class of Farmers in Selected Villages

	Rich Peasants			Poor Peasants			Landless Labour			All		
	HSR	*HWSR*	*All*	*HSR*	*HWSR*	*All*	*HSR*	*HWSR*	*All*	*HSR*	*HWSR*	*All*
1	*2*	*3*	*4*	*5*	*6*	*7*	*8*	*9*	*10*	*11*	*12*	*13*
1. Total No.of Housholds	37 (36.3)	44 (24.0)	81 (28.4)	61 (59.8)	111 (60.7)	172 (60.4)	4 (3.9)	28 (15.3)	32 (11.2)	102 (100)	183 (100)	285 (100)
2. Average No. of persons per household	9.1	5.8	7.3	5.2	4.3	4.6	4.5	3.7	3.8	6.6	4.6	5.3
3. Average No. of adults per household	6.1	3.7	4.8	3.6	2.7	3.0	2.3	2.4	2.4	4.5	2.9	3.5
4. Average No. of children per household	3.0	2.1	2.5	1.6	1.5	1.5	2.3	1.3	1.4	2.1	1.6	1.8
5. Average size of land holding per household (acres):												

(Contd.)

(Contd.)

1	2	3	4	5	6	7	8	9	10	11	12	13
Dry	9.2	5.7	7.3	2.1	1.8	1.9	-	-	-	4.6	2.5	3.2
Irrigated	1.5	2.2	1.9	0.02	0.04	0.04	-	-	-	0.5	0.5	0.6
Total	10.5	7.9	9.2	2.1	1.8	1.9	-	-	-	5.1	3.0	3.8
6. No. of households with Ruminant Livestock	37	40	77	61	80	141	4	4	8	102	124	226
7. Average no. of Ruminant Livestock per household	41.5	5.4	22.8	16.1	2.7	8.5	15.0	2.8	8.9	25.3	3.6	13.4
8. No. of households with Small Ruminants	37	-	37	61	-	61	4	-	4	102	-	102
9. Average No. of Small Ruminants per household		33.8	-	-	13.3	-	-	13.5	-	-	20.8	-

Note : Figures in the brackets are percentages to total.
HSR = Households with small ruminants.
HWSR = Households without small ruminants.

It is evident that inspite of droughtprone character of the region, the pressure of man in relation to the carrying capacity of land is much large. Poor peasants are not in a position to introduce irrigation due to their limited resources like capital. Average size of land holding per household under irrigation among the poor peasants is only 0.04 acres, as compared with 1.9 acres in the case of rich peasants. Though the villages are inhabited largely by poor and landless families (being 71.6 per cent of total households), whose socio-economic conditions are miserable, the rich peasants too are often subject to misery and scarcity conditions.

Realising the difficulties and risk involved in farming, the farmers of the region have diversified their economy into animal husbandry so as to maximise the total returns on the farm with the same physical resources. It is also clear from Table-4.2 that a large number of farmers possess ruminant livestock, which are raised mostly on resources which are free to them, *i.e.,* own labour, common property resource lands, stubbles and crop residues. It is more so in the case of sheep and goats which are raised mainly on CPRs. Only 25 per cent of the landless households possess ruminant livestock, which is mainly due to their very poor resource base. As they own no crop land and a proper house to keep the livestock, particularly large ruminants, they are reluctant to adopt animal husbandry. Also, as long as these households had an opportunity to graze their animals around their villages on CPRs, maintained the ruminant livestock on a large scale. But due to the shrinkage and degradation of CPRs they have to travel with their animals over a longer distance for grazing. Since their family size is also small and both adults and children are needed to earn their daily bread, unable to travel longer distances the whole day. On the other hand, the rich peasants both with large size of arable land and large family size including children are in a position to maintain relatively a larger size of ruminant livestock. The average size of ruminant livestock owned by the rich peasants is 22.8 animals per household as compared with poor peasants and landless households, who possess on an average 8.5 and 8.9 ruminants per household respectively (see Table-4.2).

It is the households with a large number of family members and bigger land holding size which have adopted the rearing of small ruminants. Table-4.2 shows that both average size of population and average land holding size is large among the households with small ruminants as compared with the households without small ruminants. This suggests that not only owning a large labour force supports the small ruminant activity, but the size of land holding also goes in favour of it. Even the average number of ruminant livestock owned (per household) by the households with small ruminants is large (25.3 animals) as compared with households without small ruminants (being 3.6 animals). Not only the households with small ruminants own sheep and goats, the share of large ruminants too is larger in their economies. This could be due to some extent to complementarities between small and large ruminants to some extent, but it is the larger resource base of richer households which enable them to have both small and large ruminants. Though we expect the CPRs to compensate for the landlessness or poor land resource base of other households, evidently they have the private resource base seems to play a much bigger role than CPRs in enabling households to keep more animals.

Groundnut, a rainfed Kharif crop, is the major crop grown on a large scale by all the farmers for the market. If rains are normal in a year, farmers get the second crop also. Usually horsegram or any other coarse grain is cultivated as a second crop. Many farmers grow ragi as the second crop. Area under food grains like ragi has come down to a greater extent. Even the cultivators depend on the market outside the village for purchase of foodgrains. Those with some assured irrigation through dug wells are cultivating sugarcane, paddy, onion and mulberry. Sericulture is limited only to a few farmers with some assured irrigation. More than 96 per cent of the rich peasants depend on agriculture as their main source of income, but still one can find them concentrating on different activities like animal husbandry, business, service and other allied work. About 40 per cent of the poor peasants depend on agriculture as their main source of income, whereas 54 per cent live mainly on wage earnings. Three percent and 27.3 per cent of them depend on animal husbandry as their main and subsidiary source of income respectively. As far as the landless households are concerned, they depend mostly (78 per cent of the households) on wage employment (cooly) as their main source of income. But six per cent of them have taken up animal husbandry as their main source of livelihood. Further, about 16 per cent of them also depend on animal husbandry as subsidiary source (see Table 4.3 below). This shows that the role played by animal husbandry in the economy of rural households particularly of poor and landless is not insignificant, though they are not the major holders of small ruminants in terms of their share in the total animals.

A major point which comes out of Table 4.3 is that small ruminants are important only as a subsidiary source of occupation and help in diversifying the rural economy. Even in the case of households with small ruminants, only 5.9 per cent kept them as the main occupation, and a many as 75.5 per cent kept them as a subsidiary occupation. By comparison, service and business played very minor role, and rural industry was totally absent in the surveyed villages. Under the economic environment of modernisation and tough competition from urban industry, the prospects of rural industry becoming a major source of diversification of the rural economy are dim. One the other hand, animal husbandry including ofcourse the small ruminants hold better prospects of promoting rural diversification.

Table 4.3

Number of Households (HSR and HWSR) with different Occupation in the Selected Villages

	Rich Peasants			*Poor Peasants*			*Landless Labour*			*All*		
	HSR	*HWSR*	*All*	*HSR*	*HWSR*	*All*	*HSR*	*HWSR*	*All*	*HSR*	*HWSR*	*All*
1	*2*	*3*	*4*	*5*	*6*	*7*	*8*	*9*	*10*	*11*	*12*	*13*
Main Occupation												
Agriculture	35 (94.6)	43 (97.7)	78 (96.3)	33 (54.1)	36 (32.4)	69 (40.1)	-	-	-	68 (66.7)	79 (43.2)	147 (51.6)
Cooly (Wage employment)	-	-	-	22 (36.1)	71 (64.0)	93 (54.1)	1 (25.0)	24 (85.7)	25 (78.1)	23 (22.5)	95 (51.9)	118 (41.4)
Small Ruminants	-	-	-	5 (8.2)	-	5 (2.9)	1 (25.0)	-	1 (3.1)	6 (5.9)	-	6 (2.1)
C B Cows	-	-	-	-	-	-	1 (25.0)	-	1 (3.1)	1 (1.0)	-	1 (0.4)
Service	2 (5.4)	-	2 (2.5)	-	1 (0.9)	1 (0.6)	-	2 (7.1)	2 (6.3)	2 (2.0)	3 (1.6)	5 (1.8)
Business	-	1 (2.3)	1 (1.2)	-	1 (0.9)	1 (0.6)	1 (25.0)	-	1 (3.1)	1 (1.0)	2 (1.1)	3 (1.1)

(Contd.)

(Contd.)

1	2	3	4	5	6	7	8	9	10	11	12	13
Others	-	-	-	1 (1.6)	2 (1.8)	3 (1.80)	-	2 (7.1)	2 (6.3)	1 (1.0)	4 (2.2)	5 (1.8)
Total Households	37 (100)	44 (100)	81 (100)	61 (100)	111 (100)	172 (100)	4 (100)	28 (100)	32 (100)	102 (100)	183 (100)	285 (100)
Subsidiary Occupation												
Small Ruminants	30 (81.1)	-	30 (37.0)	43 (70.5)	-	43 (25.0)	3 (75.0)	-	3 (9.4)	76 (75.5)	-	76 (26.7)
C B Cows	5 (13.5)	2 (4.5)	7 (8.6)	1 (1.6)	3 (2.7)	4 (2.3)	-	2 (7.1)	2 (6.3)	6 (5.9)	7 (3.8)	13 (4.6)
Agriculture	2 (5.4)	1 (2.3)	3 (3.7)	7 (11.5)	75 (67.6)	82 (47.7)	-	-	-	9 (8.8)	76 (41.5)	85 (29.8)
Sericulture	-	1 (2.3)	1 (1.2)	-	-	-	-	-	-	-	1 (0.50)	1 (0.4)
Service	-	1 (2.3)	1 (1.2)	-	1 (0.9)	1 (0.6)	-	-	-	-	2 (1.1)	2 (0.7)
Business	-	2 (4.5)	2 (2.5)	-	-	-	1 (25.0)	-	1 (3.1)	1 (1.0)	2 (1.1)	3 (1.1)

(Contd.)

(Contd.)

1	*2*	*3*	*4*	*5*	*6*	*7*	*8*	*9*	*10*	*11*	*12*	*13*
Cooly	-	10	10	10	25	35	-	3	3	10	38	48
		(22.7)	(12.4)	(16.4)	(22.5)	(20.4)		(10.7)	(9.4)	(9.8)	(20.8)	(16.8)
Others	-	1	1	-	3	3	-	1	1	-	5	5
		(2.3)	(1.2)		(2.7)	(1.7)		(3.6)	(3.1)		(2.7)	(1.8)
No Occupation	-	26	26	-	4	4	-	22	22	-	52	52
		(59.1)	(32.1)		(3.6)	(2.3)		(78.6)	(68.8)		(28.40)	(18.2)
Total	37	44	81	61	111	172	4	28	32	102	183	285
Households	(100)	(100)	(100)	(100)	(100)	(100)	(100)	(100)	(100)	(100)	(100)	(100)

Note : Figures in the brackets are percentages to total households in the columns.

HSR = Households with small ruminants.

HWSR = Households without small ruminants.

4.3 Composition of Livestock and Type of People Keeping Different Species in the Selected Villages

Almost all the farmers interviewed depend on the manure from ruminant livestock in the cultivation of groundnut and other crops. In the absence of this manure, the farmers would have had to depend much more on chemical fertilizers which, if exclusively or excessively used, is reported to adversely affect soil texture, apart from increasing the costs per unit of output. Draught power of the cattle is also very important in their agriculture. Out of the total households (285) in the sample villages, 32.3 per cent possess both small and large ruminants, 3.5 per cent possess only small ruminants, 43.4 per cent possess only large ruminants and the remaining 20.8 per cent possess no ruminant livestock. Among the ten households which have maintained only goats and sheep, nine households belonged to the poor peasant's class and one to the rich peasant class. All of them belonged to schedule castes. The rich peasant, who is also a teacher, has maintained a few small ruminants on hired-in labour as subsidiary source of income. It was not required for him to maintain large ruminants since his farming also depended on hired-in labour. The poor peasants could not maintain any large ruminant, since they had the problem of capital. Their landholding size was also very small and often left fallow. For them it was easier to maintain a few goats and sheep as a subsidiary source of income than to keep large ruminants. In animal husbandry the local breed of non-descript cattle dominates large ruminants and goats and sheep form the small ruminants. The role of buffaloes is very marginal. Cross-bred cows have been introduced in the villages, which are mostly raised by the rich farmers (see Table 4.4). A few poor and landless households have been given cross bred cows on loan under anti-poverty programmes, but we found that the success is marginal and in some cases even negative. It has been reported that fodder is the major cost component in the maintenance of cross bred cows which is beyond the reach of poor and landless to buy each day the required quantity. It is also said that cross bred cows are susceptible to diseases, since they need good housing and sanitation, which the poor and landless cannot afford. In the past these households use to maintain a few local cows and buffaloes, which was maintained exclusively on free grazing. As the CPRs have become eroded and reduced, it has become difficult for them to maintain even the non-descript cows. The rich farmers too expressed certain limitations towards cross-bred cows like susceptibility to diseases and non-availability of green fodder from CPRs.

It has been reported by the farmers that the population of bullocks has decreased which is due to the high overhead cost of maintaining them on crop residues and purchased fodder. But since farming depends mostly on monsoon, it is essential for them to keep the draught power always ready even now. With the start of monsoon, the demand for draught power increases and, hence, it is necessary for them to maintain either a pair of bullocks or some local cows. For the poor peasants particularly, it is essential to have the draught power ready, since they can not afford to hire bullocks or tractors unlike the rich peasants. If tillage is postponed for some days they may have to depend only on wage employment for their living. Table-4.4 shows that 36 per cent of the poor peasants have maintained bullocks mainly for their own agriculture, though they may hire them out also whenever they are free. Among the rich peasants about 78 per cent of the households own bullocks, the remaining 22 per cent find it worthwhile to hire bullocks or tractors rather than keeping them the whole year. Also, farmers without bullocks are using local cows for draught power. About 74 and 58 per cent of the rich and poor peasants respectively have maintained non-descript cows for draught power, milk and manure. Even a few landless households (about 16 per cent) have maintained non-descript cows for milk and hiring out of draught power, mostly to the

Table 4.4

Number of Households (HSR and HWSR) Keeping Different Species of Livestock in the Selected Villages

Category of Households		*Total Households*	*Bullocks*	*Local Cows*	*Cross Breed Cows*	*Buffaloes*	*Sheep*	*Goats*	*Pigs*
1	*2*	*3*	*4*	*5*	*6*	*7*	*8*	*9*	*10*
Rich Peasants	HSR	37	33 (89.2)	30 (81.0)	8 (21.6)	19 (51.4)	19 (51.4)	28 (75.7)	2 (5.4)
	HWSR	44	30 (68.2)	30 (68.2)	11 (25.0)	15 (34.1)	-	-	4 (9.1)
	All	81	63 (77.8)	60 (74.1)	19 (23.5)	34 (42.0)	19 (23.5)	28 (34.6)	6 (7.4)
Poor Peasants	HSR	61	32 (52.5)	40 (65.6)	3 (4.9)	5 (8.2)	19 (31.1)	46 (75.4)	2 (3.3)
	HWSR	111	30 (27.0)	60 (54.0)	10 (9.0)	6 (5.4)	-	-	7 (6.3)
	All	172	62 (36.0)	100 (58.1)	13 (7.6)	11 (6.4)	19 (11.0)	46 (26.7)	9 (5.2)
Landless Labour	HSR	4	-	3 (75.0)	1 (25.0)	-	-	4 (100)	-

(Contd.)

(Contd.)

1	2	3	4	5	6	7	8	9	10
	HWSR	28	1	2	2	-	-	-	-
			(3.6)	(7.10)	(7.1)				
	All	32	1	5	3	-	-	4	-
			(3.1)	(15.6)	(9.4)			(12.5)	
All	HSR	102	65	73	12	24	38	78	4
			(63.7)	(71.6)	(11.8)	(23.5)	(37.30)	(76.50)	(3.9)
	HWSR	183	61	92	23	21	-	-	11
			(33.30)	(50.30)	(12.6)	(11.5)			(6.0)
	All	285	126	165	35	45	38	78	15
			(44.20)	(57.9)	(12.3)	(15.8)	(13.3)	927.40	(5.3)

Note : Figures in the brackets are percentages to total number of households. Since many households keep more than one species of livestock their break-up overlaps.

HSR = Households with small ruminants.

HWSR = Households without small ruminants.

rich peasants (see Table 4.4 above). Rich peasants in turn provide fodder (crop residues and stubble grazing) in exchange of draught power. A system of bartering draught power within the same caste group is also found. Particularly it is more among the kith and kins and among the scheduled caste households even outside kith and kins. Either they exchange bullocks/cows or lend them in exchange for fodder.

The number of local cows has increased at the aggregate level, but at the household level it has been distributed over many families including the poor and landless unlike the concentration of large herds with the rural elites in the past. This changed composition is due to technology, changed cropping pattern, commercialisation of agriculture, shrinkage and degradation of CPRs and the diversification of household economy of the elites. This is a welcome sign as far as the rural poor is concerned. Unfortunately the village system has lost a substantial part of the CPRs on which the ruminants of the poor can survive. Table 4.4 above, shows that even now only 58 per cent of the poor peasants and 16 per cent of the landless households possess non-descript cows, as compared with the rich peasants where a large number of them (74 percent) own non-descript cows.

In the case of sheep and goats, it has been found that the population of these animals has increased, but due to the increased demand for meat, a number of animals are used for slaughter regularly. Even then the goats' population has maintained an increasing trend, due to their being more prolific than sheep. It was reported by many respondents in the surveyed villages that, atleast in the recent past, the majority of the sheep and goat keepers were poor households though a few rich farmers too had larger herds of small ruminants than the poor. Under the changed system of agriculture and the village eco-system, even the rich have now started keeping sheep and goats on a large scale. This is due to the advantage of securing cash income from small ruminants whenever needed, low investment in the rearing of sheep and goats as compared with other large ruminants, decreased fodder base (both own as well as from CPRs) making large ruminants costlier to keep, and the requirement of organic manure for their agriculture. In the rearing of small ruminants, some amount of own land goes in favour of their economies. It is particularly favourable in the case of sheep which can be grazed on stubbles after the crop is harvested, which help these animals as a good source of fodder for some months. About 24 per cent and 35 per cent of the rich peasants have maintained sheep and goats respectively. Only 11 per cent of the poor peasants have maintained sheep, and none among the landless household has maintained them. As compared with sheep, a large number of poor peasants (26.7 per cent) are keeping goats. Even the landless households (12.5 per cent) have maintained them (see Table 4.4).

Both among the rich as well as poor peasants, a large number of households with small ruminants have maintained bullocks, local cows and buffaloes as compared with the households without small ruminants. On the other hand many households without small ruminants have maintained cross bred cows and pigs as compared with the households with small ruminants. As far as the landless households are concerned, only a few with small ruminants and two households without small ruminants have reported as owning the cross bred cows. Only one household without small ruminants has owned the bullocks (see Table 4.4 above). The argument advocated by Damodaran (Damodaran, 1987) that the poor sections prefer to keep the cattle (non-descript) was not corroborated in the study villages. In fact even the common belief that sheep and goats are the symbol of poor and landless families and considering goat as the 'poor man's cow', is now in question.

Further, the system of collective grazing of livestock particularly local cows and buffaloes still exist in the study villages, though at a lower level. This could be one of the reasons which enables many households to maintain one or two non-descript cows and buffaloes. There are a few common herdsmen in the village who collect the cows or buffaloes of different households in the morning, graze them in one herd over widely spread CPRs and bring them back to the owner's house in the evening. The common herder collect the fee from the owners of animals ranging from Rs. 10 per cow to Rs. 20 per buffaloe per month. In the absence of collective grazing of non-descript cows and buffaloes by common herdsmen, many households would not have had maintained such animals on own labour. In the case of goats and sheep such an arrangement of common herdsmen is becoming uncommon. The reason being that the common herdsmen would get much less (only around Rs. 40 to Rs. 80 per flock/herd of 20 to 40 animals per annum) as fee for grazing small ruminants. Also, goats and sheep need much more care and attention against theft and predators than in the case of non-descript cows and buffaloes. Further, since many households in the study villages have a surplus of own labour including that of the children and the aged, which is used in the rearing of goats and sheep.

5

ECONOMIC RETURNS FROM SMALL RUMINANTS

5.1 Introduction

This chapter, the core part of the study begins by analysing what role small ruminants play in the economy of the rural households in terms of income earned. Using different concepts of costs and returns which are explained earlier (Chapter 2), we analyse how they vary across different classes of households and different flock sizes of animals. This helps us in identifying the optimal size yielding highest net returns, which can be compared with the average size of animal holding in different classes. We will also analyse the characteristics of more efficient rearers of small ruminants as against inefficient households. Finally, we also analyse the composition of income from small ruminants. All this enables us to understand different facets of the economics of small ruminants. While in this chapter, we have combined sheep and goats together as small ruminants, in the next we have analysed them separately for comparison between them. While estimating the costs and gross returns, we have used the 1987-88 prices.

It may be recalled here that rural households use free inputs like free fodder from CPRs and own labour in rearing ruminants. We have tried to analyse how the economics of small ruminants is affected in different conceptual situations—when the free inputs are not valued, and when they are valued. The free fodder from CPRs is not a personal cost even when imputed but a social cost. It would be interesting to see how the economics is affected under the most comprehensive concepts of costs inclusive of social costs, imputed cost of own labour, and risk premium on small ruminants. Most households do not pass this rigorous test of economic costs, and the small ruminant economy seems to thrive on free inputs. However, in the long run all costs have to be recovered if the small ruminant economy has to be viable and sustainable.

5.2 Role of Small Ruminants in Household Economy

In order to assess the contribution of sheep and goats to total household income, we begin by analysing the share from different sources in the value of total gross returns of the household across different classes. By gross returns we mean the value of goods produced in different sectors before deducting any costs. The importance of costs varies between sectors, paid out costs, for example, being significant in cultivation but not in small ruminants. Because of the differing importance of costs, it is useful to analyse the relative roles of different sectors of the household economy that bring returns to it, both in terms of value of gross product and net produce or net returns. We have used the term 'gross returns' instead of 'product' mainly because it is also inclusive of wage income and salaries earned by the households. The share of different sources in the total gross returns of households across different classes is presented in Table 5.1 and also in Diagram 5.1.

The rich peasants try to maintain their higher total income both from agriculture as well as from other subsidiary sources like animal husbandry, business, service etc. Yield from agricultural crops of these farmers is also better as compared with the other class of farmers. Though agriculture contributes a lot (63.6 per cent) to their total gross returns, animal husbandry also occupies an important place in their economy. Its share in total household returns was around 34 per cent. Sheep and goats are not a major source of income to these households, even then more than 12 per cent of the total gross returns come from these animals. As the study region is prone to crop failures, and it is difficult to maintain large ruminants

Table 5.1

Percentage Share of Gross Returns from Different Sources Among the Households with Small Ruminants in the Selected Villages

Category of Households	*Crop Cultivation*	*Large Ruminants*	*Small Ruminants*	*Hiring out of own labour*	*Other Sources*	*Total Income*
			Per cent			
Rich Peasants	63.6	21.5	12.4	0	2.5	100
Poor Peasants	41.3	19.0	17.3	22.0	0.3	100
Landless Labour	0	38.9	24.4	32.7	3.9	100
All	55.6	21.0	14.1	7.4	1.8	100

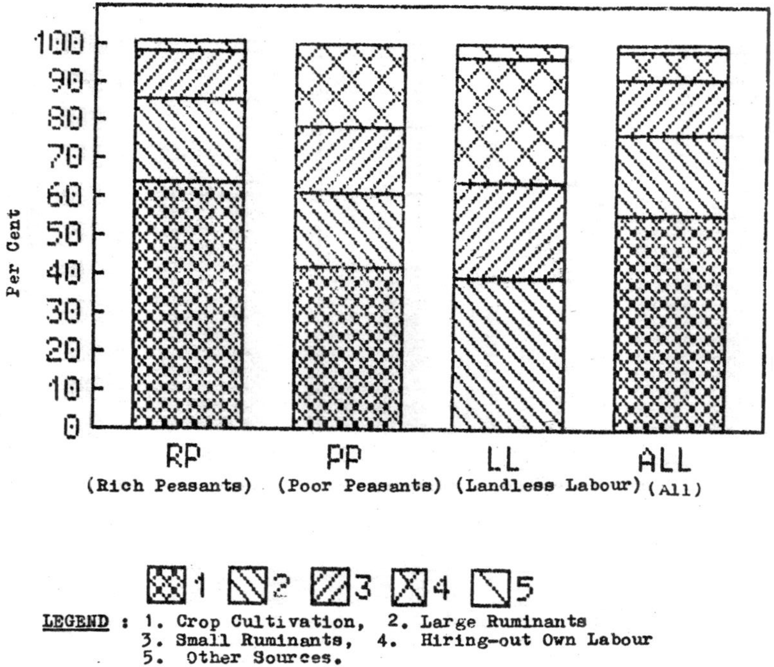

Diagram 5.1

Percentage Share of Gross Returns from Different Sources to Total Gross Returns Among the Households with Small Ruminants in the Selected Villages

during such periods, even these households are concentrating to a large extent on sheep and goats, which need minimum water and fodder and survive on available CPRs.

It is interesting however that though the share of rich peasants in small ruminants across classes, *i.e.*, in the village total is large. The share of ruminants in the household economy of rich peasants is smaller than that of poor peasants. Though poor peasants have a minor share in small ruminants as seen in our last chapter, the relative importance of small ruminants is greater in their economy.

In the economy of poor peasants, animal husbandry's share to total household return was substantial (36.3 per cent) which was very important for them. Since the share of agriculture to their total gross return was less (41.3 per cent), than in the case of rich peasants, poor peasants' livelihood has to be supplemented by income from animal husbandry more than in the case of the rich peasants. For rich peasants, income from animal husbandry was more a source of making savings and investment than a source of subsistence. Poor peasants own some land, but due to its poor quality and complete dependence on rainfall for its cultivation, they are not in a position even to take one successful dry crop annually. During droughts when the income and employment from crop cultivation and large ruminants become uncertain, these households concentrate to a large extent on sheep and goats. The degraded condition of CPRs has also forced them to concentrate on small ruminants rearing as the dependable proposition, though they may not keep large herds. Poor peasants consider sheep and goats rearing as a source of subsistence and as insurance against risk. More than 17 per cent of their gross returns constituted the share from small ruminants in their case.

The landless households depend to a large extent on animal husbandry for their household consumption requirements. Around 64 per cent of their total gross returns constituted the share from animal husbandry. Thus the relative importance of animal husbandry in their household economy turned out to be higher than that of even wage labour. Within animal husbandry, however, large ruminants played a more important role mainly through milk. The share of small ruminants in their total gross return was 24.4 percent, compared to 38.9 per cent from large ruminants. However, even the role of small ruminants in their household economy was greatest in the case of landless labour as compared to both other classes. As economic status and possession of land declines, the relative importance of sheep and goats increases considerably across classes of rural households.

Gross returns do not reflect the economic viability of the concerned economic activities, since a substantial proportion of gross return may go out as cost of the inputs purchased. Also, when the values of gross outputs from different sectors are added to arrive at the total, there is a certain amount of double counting at the household level, when the output of one sector (such as manure from animal husbandry) forms an input in another sector (such as cultivation) of the same household economy. When net returns are considered, such a problem is avoided. Thus, net returns over input costs have also to be considered while discussing the importance of different sources of income in the household economy. While estimating the share of net returns from different sources in the total net returns of the household, we have taken into account only costs A2, since they are comparable across sources and free from arbitrariness inherent in any imputation.

It can be seen from Table 5.2 that the share of small ruminants is even larger in terms of net returns in the economy of households than in terms of gross returns, and what is more, their relative importance is even greater for landless labour. Thus the picture about the role of small ruminants becomes even sharper. Across class of rural households, it is much more in the case of poor peasants and landless labour

Table 5.2

Percentage Share of Net Returns (Gross Returns minus cost A2) from Different Sources to Total Net Returns Among the Households with Small Ruminants in the Selected Villages

Category of Households	*Crop Cultivation*	*Large Ruminants*	*Small Ruminants*	*Hiring out of Own Labour*	*Other Sources*	*Total Returns*
			Per cent			
Rich Peasants	63.4	15.0	17.9	0	3.7	100
Poor Peasants	36.8	13.9	21.0	27.9	0.4	100
Landless Labour	0	24.2	29.1	41.7	5.0	100
All	53.1	14.8	19.1	10.4	2.6	100

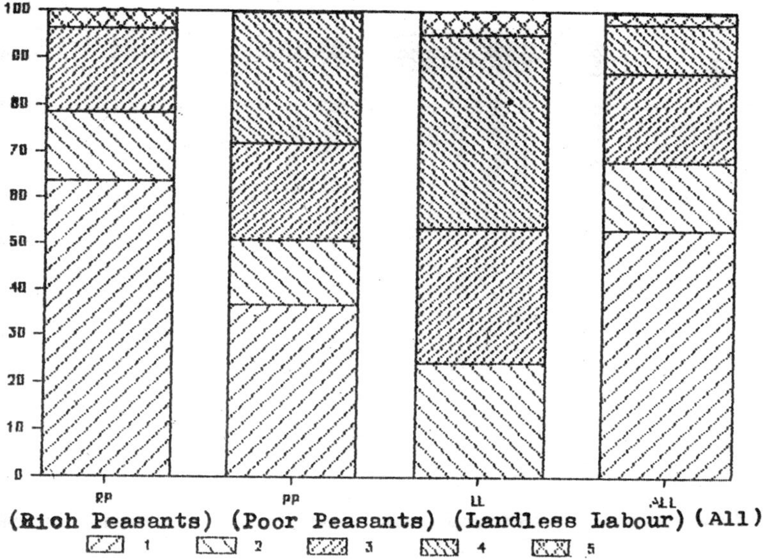

LEGEND : 1. Crop Cultivation, 2. Large Ruminants
3. Small Ruminamts, 4. Hiring-out Own Labour
5. Other Sources.

Diagram 5.2

Percentage Share of Net Returns (Gross Returns Minus Cost A2) from Different Sources to Total Net Returns among the Households with Small Ruminants in the Selected Villages

households, being 21 and 29.1 per cent respectively. Moreover, net returns from small ruminants are more than from large ruminants among all classes, which was not so in terms of gross returns. This is suggestive of the greater role played by free fodder in the case of small ruminants, while purchased fodder is not insignificant in the case of large ruminants. In the case of landless labour households, the other major source of income is hiring-out of their own labour, being 41.7 per cent of their total net returns. The share of large ruminants too is substantial in their economies (see Diagram 5.2).

5.3 Net Returns from Crop Cultivation

Net returns over different costs will give us an idea to assess the economic viability of a particular sector and also the constraints on it. Though our focus is on the economics of small ruminants, we have also tried to present in brief the costs and returns from crop cultivation and large ruminants. Households with an easy access to certain inputs like own farm yard manure, draught power, seeds etc. are able to get good returns from crop cultivation, both per acre as well as per farm. Table 5.3 shows that cost A1 is high both per acre as well as per household in the case of rich peasants but they incur less of cost C1 per acre as compared with poor peasants[8].

Table 5.3

Costs and Gross Returns (Rs.) from Crop Cultivation Per Year

		Costs			Gross Returns
		A1	*A2*	*C1*	
Rich Peasants:	Per household	6999	6999	8240	21479
	Per acre	654	654	769	2006
Poor Peasants:	Per household	1194	1208	1695	4036
	Per acre	568	575	807	1921
All :	Per household	2386	3395	4166	10622
	Per acre	633	634	779	1985

8. The cost concepts used here have been discussed already in chapter 2.

Though cost C1 per acre is higher in the case of poor peasants, the returns per acre are less as compared with the rich peasants. This is because of the inclusion of the imputed cost of family labour in cost C1, which is used relatively abundantly per acre on small farms, going beyond the point of equality between market wage and marginal product of labour. The gross returns could be higher on larger farms because an easy and timely access to certain key inputs has helped the rich peasants to use more of them, reflected in higher costs A1 per acre on the farms of rich peasants. Interestingly, net returns per acre over cost A1 are same for both rich as well as poor peasants, being Rs. 1352 and Rs. 1353, respectively. It is only over Cost C1 that net returns per acre in the case of poor peasants are lower (Rs. 1114) as compared with the rich peasants (Rs. 1237) (see Table 5.4 below). The excess use of family labour in crop cultivation by the poor peasants was due to the low opportunity cost of such labour.

Table 5.4

Net Returns (Rs.) from Crop Cultivation Using Different Cost Concepts

		Net returns over cost		
		A1	*A2*	*C1*
Rich Peasants:	Per household	14480	14480	13239
	Per acre	1352	1352	1237
Poor Peasants:	Per household	2842	2828	2341
	Per acre	1353	1346	1114
All :	Per household	7236	7227	6456
	Per acre	1352	1351	1206

5.4 Net Returns from Large Ruminants

The costs and returns from large ruminants are worked out to make a brief comparison with crop cultivation and rearing of small ruminants. The returns from large ruminants are inclusive of the imputed value of own bullock used on farms as draught power (after taking into account the bullock days), the apportioned value of bullock labour hired-out (after deducting wage rate for manual labour without bullock), the imputed value is organic manure used on own farm, value of such manure sold to others, and value of milk and milk products consumed at source and sold. (see Table 5.5 for composition of gross returns from large ruminants).

Table 5.5

Different Components of Gross Returns from Large Ruminants Across Class of Rural Households

(Rs. per household)

	Rich Peasants	*Poor Peasants*	*Landless Labour*	*All*
1. Net Change in the Value of Stock (Mainly Organic Increase)	464 (6.4)	97 (5.2)	300 (12.0)	238 (6.2)
2. Sale of animals	-	47 (2.5)	-	28 (0.8)
3. Imputed value of Draught-power used on own farm	2576 (35.4)	734 (39.6)	-	1373 (35.7)
4. Draught Power hired-out	24 (0.3)	243 (13.1)	-	154 (4.0)
5. Manure	897 (12.4)	248 (13.4)	200 (8.0)	481 (12.5)
6. Milk, Ghee, etc.	3309 (45.5)	486 (26.2)	1994 (80.0)	1569 (40.8)
7. Total	7270 (100)	1855 (100)	2494 (100)	3843 (100)

Among the different components of gross returns per household from large ruminants, share of milk and ghee is substantial, being 40.8 per cent. The only other major component of gross returns is the imputed value of draught power used on own farm. Across class of farmers income from hiring-out of draught power is important in the case of poor peasants which constitute 13.1 per cent of their total returns from large ruminants, whereas it is negligible in the case of rich peasants. In other words draught animals are maintained by the rich peasants only to use them on own farms, whereas poor peasants maintained them for use on own farm as well as to get income by hiring them out. Further, landless labour households have maintained one or two cross-bred cows each, and hence the share of milk and ghee to their total gross returns from large ruminants is substantial (being 80.0 per cent). Nevertheless, even among the rich peasants the share of milk and ghee to their total gross returns from large ruminants is substantial (see Table 5.5).

Though the cost concepts have been slightly modified by us for use in animal husbandry, we have not gone into the details of the economics of large ruminants here. For instance, in large ruminants the cost on account of risk premium has not been included as in the case of small ruminants. Comparisons are, however, made in terms of comparable cost concepts. Further, economics of different species like buffaloes, cattle and cross-bred cows has not been worked out separately within large ruminants in detail. Since in the study region we find only a few buffaloes and cross bred cows, they have been taken together with cattle while calculating the costs and returns from large ruminants. Nevertheless, this analysis is relevant, so that the importance and viability of the large ruminants sector can be assessed and compared with other household sectors.

Looking at table 5.6, we can see that the gross returns from large ruminants per animal in the study region as a whole are significant. Across class of farmers, it is the landless who are getting the highest gross returns per animal. This may be because, having no land, they spend more on purchased fodder/concentrates, reflected in higher cost A1. Due to the dependence on purchased inputs, they are also more choosy in keeping animals, while the rich peasants keep a lot of unproductive animals also.

Gross returns per animal are the lowest among poor peasants. They incur less of cost A1 (neither own fodder nor purchased fodder/concentrates are used sufficiently). As compared with the rich peasants, poor peasants incur more of own labour cost reflected in higher Cost C1 and Cost Cs than cost A1 per animal. The marginal product of this higher cost is evidently low, since it is not reflected in higher gross return from large ruminants. It appears that the economics of large ruminants is significantly responsive to improved variety of fodder and concentrates. Further, the gross returns per household from large ruminants are substantial (being Rs. 7,270) in the case of rich peasants as compared with poor peasants and the landless (being Rs. 1855 and 2494, respectively). This is only because the rich peasants own more large ruminants rather than due to higher returns per animal.

Let us have a look at the net returns from large ruminants over different costs across different class of farmers. Net returns per household as well as per animal over cost C1 and Cs are negative in the case of poor peasants. Since poor peasants incur more of C1 and Cs, the net returns are negative. But in practice, as both imputed costs of own labour and grazing on common lands included in C1 and Cs respectively are free to them, they consider it economical to maintain large ruminants even with these costs. The cost of grazing is a social cost borne by the society and hence individual owner of the animals does not consider it as a cost. Since cost C1 is inclusive of the own labour cost and the opportunity cost of such labour is zero/negligible, they consider it also as free. On the other hand, both rich peasants and landless households have net positive returns per household as well as per animal, in respect of all cost concepts (see Table 5.7 for details).

This brings out the fact that in the absence of free grazing, keeping large ruminants will become costly and non-viable

Table 5.6

Costs and Gross Returns (Rs.) from Large Ruminants Per Year

		Costs					*Gross Returns*
		A1	*A2*	*B1*	*C1*	*Cs*	
Rich Peasants:	Per household	2974	2974	3830	6000	7070	7270
	Per animal	379	379	489	766	902	928
Poor Peasants:	Per household	543	543	786	2397	2761	1855
	Per animal	196	196	284	885	997	670
Landless Labour:	Per household	965	965	1274	1813	2018	2494
	Per animal	643	643	849	1209	1345	1663
All:	Per household	1442	1442	1909	3681	4295	3845
	Per animal	316	316	419	807	942	843

Table 5.7

Net Returns (Rs.) from Large Ruminants Using Different Cost Concepts

		Net Returns Over Cost				
		A1	*A2*	*B1*	*C1*	*Cs*
Rich Peasants:	Per household	4296	4296	3440	1270	200
	Per animal	549	549	439	162	26
Poor Peasants:	Per household	1312	1312	1069	-542	-906
	Per animal	474	474	386	-195	-327
Landless Labour:	Per household	1529	1529	1220	681	476
	Per animal	1020	1020	814	454	318
All :	Per household	2403	2403	1936	164	-450
	Per animal	527	527	424	36	-99

for the poor peasants. If the cost of own labour is also included it will be an uneconomic proposition for them. On the other hand even if the rich peasants are charged for the use of free grazing lands (CPRs), it may not affect the economic viability of keeping large ruminants in their case. In turn it may increase the returns from large ruminants because they would then weed out unproductive cattle, and more fodder would be available per animal from CPRs.

5.5 Gross Returns from Small Ruminants and their Composition

We have explained in the Chapter 2 above how returns from animal husbandry are calculated and their components (p. 35). While estimating the gross returns from animal husbandry, we have also taken into account the organic increase *i.e.*, net change in the value of the stock during one year period. The other sources of gross returns from animal husbandry are sale of animals, manure, wool, skins, milk and the returns from the sale of dead animals. Share of organic increase (in value terms) to total gross returns from small ruminants was highest, being 53.2 per cent, which is nothing but an addition to the stock and hence accumulation and capital formation. But it is through sale of animals that the sheep and goats keepers get regular cash income, which amounts to 33.5 per cent of the total returns from small ruminants. Though this may look as disinvestment of the stock, maintaining adult males, aged and sick animals beyond a certain level adds to total cost rather than to returns. By culling such animals, apart from reducing the cost and risk the rearers can meet their immediate household cash requirements like education of their children, input cost of other household sectors like crop cultivation etc. It could be a disinvestment only when young and productive animals are sold. It would be optimal to keep the animal till the rate of organic increase remains higher than the opportunity cost of waiting in terms of interest on the capital (the animal) as valued in the beginning of the year. When the organic increase has stopped or is negligible, the animal is ready for sale unless its current production in the form of milk or wool is more than the normal interest from the animal.

Across class of farmers, it is the rich peasants who gain much in terms of both increase in the stock (organic increase) as well as by way of selling their animals (see Table 5.8 below for details). As it has been mentioned elsewhere, the stock size possessed by the rich peasants is large and hence the organic increase of their stock is also high. Since their household requirements are met out of other means like business, crop cultivation etc., they are not forced to sell the animals at a lower price. Their bargaining power in the market is also high. On the other hand poor peasants and landless households, whose stock base is also very low and are not in a position to meet their immediate cash requirements (as their economy is less diversified), are compelled to sell even the young and productive animals with very low bargaining power.

As a whole the value of manure (both imputed as well as sold) constitute around 8 per cent of the total returns from small ruminants. Actually its contribution is much more. Land owning households have reported the increase in the yield of agricultural crops as a result of the application of small ruminants' manure to crop lands. Its use has also brought down the cost of cultivation. Even the landless households have earned both cash income as well as fodder (crop residues and stubble grazing), by way of exchanging small ruminants' manure to the rich peasants. Returns from wool, skin and milk are very marginal (being 0.55 per cent of the gross returns per household).

Table 5.8

Different Components of Gross Returns from Small Ruminants Across Class of Farmers (Rs. per household)

	Rich Peasants	*Poor Peasants*	*Landless Households*	*All*
1. Net Change in the value of stock (mainly organic increase)	2300 (54.8)	851 (50.4)	963 (61.5)	1381 (53.2)
2. Sale of animals	1318 (31.4)	625 (37.0)	463 (29.6)	870 (33.5)
3. Wool	2 (0.04)	0.4 (0.03)	-	0.9 (0.04)
4. Manure	318 (7.6)	137 (8.1)	139 (8.9)	203 (7.8)
5. Skin	25 (0.6)	6 (0.4)	-	13 (0.5)
6. Milk	-	0.4 (0.03)	-	0.2 (0.01)
7. Income from dead animals	235 (5.6)	70 (4.1)	-	127 (4.9)
8. Total	4198 (100)	1690 (100)	1564 (100)	2595 (100)

Note : Figures in the brackets are percentages.

5.6 Net Returns from Small Ruminants

Though there exists a wide market for small ruminants and their products in India, the economics of these animals has not been studied in detail. The sheep and goats raisers too hardly calculate the cost and returns from these animals, unlike from crop cultivation. Maintaining sheep and goats depends on the extent and availability of free/cheap labour and fodder. Free labour indicates own family labour used usually with zero or negligible opportunity cost. Labour is cheap since the wages paid for hired labour in the case of small ruminants are also very low, unlike in the case of crop cultivation where cost of hired labour is much more. Free fodder constitutes the unused dry grass, thorns, bushes etc. from CPRs and the stubbles on which small ruminants survive and the owner of the flock/herd pays nothing for their use. If we look at Table 5.9, imputed cost of own labour accounts for more than half of the total costs, being 61 per cent for all households together and as high as 68.6 per cent in the case of poor peasants. Imputed interest on capital and imputed cost of fodder obtained from CPRs are the next biggest items, accounting for 16.1 and 14.3 per cent in the case of all households together. In contrast, paid out costs including rent paid on leased-in animals accounted for less than 4 per cent of total costs.

Table 5.9

Composition of Costs in the Rearing of Small Ruminants Across Class of Farmers

(Rs. per household)

	Rich Peasants	*Poor Peasants*	*Landless Households*	*All*
1. Paid out cost (cash and kind)	120 (3.1)	50 (2.1)	108 (6.1)	78 (2.7)
2. Rent paid on leased-in animals	19 (0.5)	31 (1.3)	-	25 (0.9)
3. Interest on capital (livestock)	772 (20.0)	290 (12.3)	294 (16.5)	465 (16.1)
4. Imputed cost of own labour used	2075 (53.6)	1620 (68.6)	1004 (56.2)	1761 (61.0)
5. Risk premium	235 (6.1)	91 (3.9)	88 (4.9)	143 (5.0)
6. Imputed cost of grazing on CPRs	647 (16.7)	279 (11.8)	290 (16.3)	413 (14.3)
7. Total cost	3868 (100)	2361 (100)	1784 (100)	2885 (100)

Note : Figures in the brackets are percentages to total cost.

If net returns are calculated taking into account the imputed cost of own labour and the imputed cost of free grazing, the rearers may not consider it economical and viable to maintain sheep and goats. As far as the economic logic is concerned, any enterprise should meet all the input costs used in the production process, out of the total returns. Economic viability of a proposition could be achieved when net returns (gross returns minus all costs) are positive. One can make a distinction between *net economic return* and *net financial return* in many propositions where free inputs are used. If net financial returns over all paid out costs are negative the proposition is not viable even in the short run, and the enterprise caught in such a situation cannot survive. On the other hand if the net economic return *i.e.*, gross returns minus all costs including imputed cost of free inputs, is negative, the enterprise may be inefficient and unsustainable in the long run, but is still viable in the short run and can survive since it has used free inputs whose opportunity costs are zero/negligible. For long term economic efficiency and sustainability of the enterprise, it is essential that all the costs including imputed costs are met.

There is need for a further clarification about the imputed cost of free grazing. It is insisted here that these costs too should be met in the long run, because that suggests a situation where fodder which is free today can be paid for tomorrow, and still the economy based on it can thrive. In other words, CPRs can be managed for sustainable and productive use and their costs can be charged to the users in such a situation. If however, there is no management of CPRs at all, and high returns are used only for private benefit without regenerating CPRs, even the high returns that meet imputed cost of free fodder, by themselves do not automatically ensure sustainable use of CPRs and long run sustainability of the small ruminant economy. Another implication is that if the returns from small ruminants are not high enough to cover such imputed costs, the cost of regeneration and sustainable management of CPRs may have to be subsidised and cannot be charged fully to users. We shall discuss this point further when we come to policy implications in the concluding chapter.

Table 5.10 shows that taking into account all households together, the total cost (cost Cs) is so high both per household and per animal that it exceeds total gross returns. If this cost has to be actually paid, the sheep and goat keepers will have to dis-invest their stock. In practice, they take into account only cost A2 which is marginal when compared with the total returns. Only rich peasants get gross returns above cost Cs, but not other classes. Hence we have also used cost concepts-Br, C1 and Cr. It may be recalled that Br includes risk premium but excludes imputed cost of family labour and imputed value of free grazing; while C1 corresponds to C1 of traditional cost concept in cultivation and includes family labour but excludes risk premium as well as free grazing. Cr includes both risk premium and imputed value of family labour, but excludes free grazing. The Table 5.10 reveals that taking all households together, cost Cr is covered by gross returns, but not in the case of poor peasants who cover only cost Br but not C1. But imputed costs are an income or a surplus to the family members. Further, cost Cs is inclusive of the cost borne by the society at large. Individual herder presently pays nothing towards this cost, though in the long run each one has to pay in terms of decreased returns from small ruminants as a result of the tragedy of the commons (Hardin, 1968). We stress even at the cost of repetition that an accounting of this cost is needed even if in an approximate way to see if a margin exists over this cost, and if at least a part of the cost could be recovered from the herders to maintain CPRs in a healthy and sustainable way. The Table 5.10 shows that rich peasants can pay such a charge if not other classes. If we look at Table 5.11 net returns over cost Cs are negative across all other types of households except in the case of rich peasants where it is positive. Goats and sheep keepers however can stay on this activity because costs A1, A2, B1 and Br are easily covered in all the cases. They can stay even if cost C1 is reckoned, since cost C1 is also income to the households. However, if the small ruminant economy has to be sustainable in the long run, institutional arrangements are necessary for sustainable use and management of CPRs and their productivity has to be enhanced, and all households will have to contribute their might in achieving this task.

Table 5.10

Costs and Gross Returns (Rs) from Small Ruminants Per Year

	Average flock/herd size per household		*Costs*							*Gross Returns*
			A1	*A2*	*B1*	*Br*	*C1*	*Cr*	*Cs*	
Rich Peasants	34	Per household	109	128	900	1135	2975	3210	3858	4198
		Per animal	3	4	26	33	86	93	112	123
Poor Peasants	14	Per household	50	81	371	462	1991	2082	2361	1690
		Per animal	3	5	25	32	139	145	165	118
Landless Labour	14	Per household	108	108	402	490	1406	1494	1784	1564
		Per animal	7	7	28	34	98	104	125	110
All	22	Per household	74	99	564	708	2325	2468	2881	2595
		Per animal	3	4	26	32	108	114	133	121

Table 5.11

Net Returns (Rs) from Small Ruminants Using Different Cost Concepts

		Net Returns Over Costs						
		A1	*A2*	*B1*	*Br*	*C1*	*Cr*	*Cs*
Rich Peasants	Per household	4089	4070	3298	3063	1223	988	340
	Per animal	120	119	97	90	37	30	11
Poor Peasants	Per household	1640	1609	1319	1228	-301	-392	-671
	Per animal	115	113	93	86	-21	-27	-47
Landless Labour	Per household	1456	1456	1162	1074	158	70	-220
	Per animal	103	103	82	76	12	6	-15
All	Per household	2521	2496	2031	1887	270	127	-286
	Per animal	118	117	95	89	13	7	-12

Along with the imputed quantity of fodder grazed on CPRs the other key input used in this activity is labour. With the help of a linear regression model *i.e.* $y = f(a + b_1x_1 + b_2x_2 \ldots\ldots\ldots b_nx_n + e)$, we have tried to estimate that more than 65 per cent variation in total returns from small ruminants is accounted for by labour cost (X1) and quantity of fodder grazed by sheep and goats on CPRs (X2) (see Table 5.12 below).

Table 5.12

Regression Equations

With Gross Returns (Rs.) as Dependent Variable

	X_1	X_2	R^2
Rich Peasants	0.45411**	569.400*	0.770166
	(1.7557)	(7.7844)	
Poor Peasants	0.37611**	152.587*	0.22738
	(3.2659)	(2.8181)	
All	0.565009*	469.5159*	0.65908
	(4.33295)	(10.8465)	

Note : X_1 = Total Cost of Labour (Rs.)

X_2 = Quantity (Tonnes) of fodder grazed on CPRs.

Figures in the brackets are 't' values.

* : Significant at 1 per cent level.

** : Significant at 5 per cent level.

Table 5.12 also shows that the marginal value product (MVP) of fodder is substantial, being Rs. 469 per tonne (for all households) and statistically significant at one per cent level. That is to say, as one additional tonne of fodder from CPRs is consumed, the output from small ruminants increases by 469 rupees. This confirms the fact that in small ruminants activity CPRs play a very important role and hence the scope to increase the productivity of CPRs through proper management and care. Interestingly, MVP of fodder from CPRs is much more in the case of rich peasants (Rs. 569) as compared with the poor peasants (Rs. 153). Since it suggests that rich peasants derive more benefits from CPRs in absolute terms, there is a justification for a charge for this use which can contribute towards better management and regeneration of CPRs.

It can be seen from Table 5.12 that labour used in the rearing of small ruminants does not pay for itself, in the sense that as one more rupee worth of labour is used, it adds less than a rupee worth of output. This also indicates excess use of labour beyond strictly economic viability in this activity. Such a situation is normally interpreted as one of disguised employment. Since, however, the opportunity cost of own labour is zero/negligible it becomes viable for them even with its low marginal value product. Surprisingly, even rich peasants who depend more on hired labour than own labour have a mvp of labour which is less than 1. This may be because human labour is hired specially for small ruminants and the herd size is less than optimal, in the sense that full utilisation of labour employed is not made.

5.7 Variations in Returns Across Flock Size

Returns from animal husbandry depend, apart from other things, on the size of animal stock that a household operates. We can make a distinction between a viable size and optimal size from the point of view of the household. A viable size should cover paid out cost, risk premium and at least the imputed cost of family labour (which means that all labour can be paid for), even if imputed cost of grazing is not covered. In other words, it is the flock/herd size for which gross returns cover cost Cr if not Cost Cs. The optimum size is that for which the net returns are maximised. The viable and optimum size of animal stock may, however, vary from place to place, from one type of management to the other and depend also on the species of animals involved. For example, in many semi-arid and hilly areas with transhumance system of grazing, the viable size of flock/herd could be different as compared with other regions with semi-intensive system of grazing.

We have tried here to assess the variations in returns across different size of small ruminants stock in the study region in terms of net returns using different cost concepts. Before doing so, the total households with different flock/herd sizes are grouped into three categories: (1) households with flock/herd size upto 10 animals, (2) households maintaining sheep and goats between 11 and 30, and (3) those households who have maintained more than 31 animals. It has been found that gross returns per animal are much more for the flock/herd size of upto 10 animals than for the flock/herd size of more than 10 animals (see Table 5.13). But if we take into account the different costs involved in realising the gross returns, it will give us a different picture. Table 5.14 shows that net returns over cost A1, A2, B1 and Br are positive and substantial when the stock constitute upto 10 animals as compared with the other units of flock/herd sizes. If the cost of own labour, cost on account of risk involved and the cost of fodder grazed on CPRs are also taken into account, net returns are positive only when the flock/herd size constitute more than 31 animals. As we have mentioned earlier, the important key inputs used in the rearing of small ruminants are labour and fodder from CPRs, these inputs are of crucial importance in the economics of small ruminants. In terms of the rigorous criterion of covering all costs for economic efficiency, it is the flock/herd size constituting more than 31 animals, which appear to be desirable. But one can also argue that the flock/herd size of up to 10 animals could also be viable where net returns (Gross returns minus paid out cost) is higher as long as the sheep and goats keepers do not incur any 'out of the pocket' expenses on the key inputs. If it is desired to achieve economic efficiency, flock/herd size should constitute more than 31 animals. This may bring economic efficiency along with the efficiency of labour but it may further increase the cost on the environment. That is, as the flock/herd size increases total social cost (cost Cs) will also increase and may further strain the CPRs. How one can use and manage these CPRs in a sustainable way along with achieving economic efficiency in small ruminants activity is a challenge at the grass root level.

Table 5.13

Costs and Gross Returns (Rs.) Per Animal from Small Ruminants Across Flock/Herd Size Per Year

Flock/herd	*No. of House-holds*	*Average flock/ herd size per Household*	*Costs*							*Gross Returns*
			A1	*A2*	*B1*	*Br*	*C1*	*Cr*	*Cs*	
Upto 10	31	5	6	10	32	40	226	233	252	181
11 to 30	48	19	2	5	25	32	127	133	153	115
31 & above	23	50	3	3	25	32	76	82	102	117
All	102	22	3	4	26	32	108	114	133	121

Table 5.14

Net Returns (Rs.) Per Animal from Small Ruminants Using Different Cost Concepts Across Flock/Herd Size

Flock/herd	*Net Returns Over Costs*						
	A1	*A2*	*B1*	*Br*	*C1*	*Cr*	*Cs*
Upto 10	175	171	149	141	-45	-52	-71
11 to 30	113	110	90	83	-12	-18	-38
31 & above	114	114	92	85	41	35	15
All	118	117	95	89	13	7	-12

5.8 Flock/Herd Size and the Optimum Returns

The tabulation of data alone does not reveal the optimum properly. We need to use regression analysis for this purpose. Thereby we also try to obtain the range of flock/herd size where positive net return can be expected, so that the range of viable size can be obtained.

The optimum level of returns are achieved when marginal cost curve intersects with the marginal revenue curve from below. Beyond this intersection the marginal cost would be above marginal revenue. It was first tried here to identify the flock/herd size at which the optimum level of returns are achieved by assuming a quadratic relationship between total returns and flock size and total costs and flock size. Since the quadratic did not give meaningful results, an attempt is made to relate total returns and total cost with flock/herd size by using a cubic relationship, except in the case of TCBr, where we have used the linear relationship since the cubic also did not give meaningful results, as follows:

1. $TR = a_1 + b_1 X + C_1 X^2 + d_1 X^3 + e$
2. $TCr = a_2 + b_2 X + C_2 X^2 + d_2 X^3 + e$
3. $TCs = a_3 + b_3 X + C_3 X^2 + d_3 X^3 + e$
4. $TCBr = a_4 + b_4 X + e$

where:

TR = Total returns (Gross) from small ruminants during one year period.

TCr = Total cost including cost on account of risk premium, excluding social cost of free grazing on CPRs.

TCs = Total cost including social cost in terms of grazing on CPRs.

TCBr = Total cost excluding the imputed cost of own labour and the imputed cost of free grazing on CPRs, but including the cost on account of risk premium.

X = Flock / herd size.

The parameters of the relationship are presented in Table 5.15 below:

Table 5.15

Regression Co-efficients

	Constant	X	X^2	X^3	R^2
TR	625.7965	47.31392***	1.762960*	-0.01029*	0.79300
		(1.62087)	(2.49440)	(-2.48791)	
TCr	554.2129	133.6019*	-1.69620*	0.009180*	0.58818
		(5.0449)	(-2.6453)	(2.4466)	
TCs	555.7823	152.9501*	-1.68779*	0.009058*	0.702809
		(5.75733)	(-2.6239)	(2.40648)	
TCBr	45.66066	31.07860*	-	-	0.846976
		(23.52642)			

Note : 't' Values are in the brackets.

* = Significant at one percent level.

** = Significant at five per cent level.

*** = Significant at ten per cent level.

Based on total costs and total returns an attempt is made to identify the range of operation for the operator to obtain positive net returns. The intercept for total costs (TCBr) function is lower than the intercept for total returns. Hence identification of the range of positive net returns by equating TR-TCBr does not arise. The range of operation is obtained by equating TR-TCr=0 and TR-TCs=0, for the cubic equations of TR-TCr and TR-TCs.

I TR - TCr = 0

$$TR = 625.7965 + 47.31392\ X + 1.62960\ X^2 - 0.01029\ X^3$$

$$Tcr = 554.2129 + 133.6019\ X - 1.69620X^2 + 0.00918\ X^3$$

$$TR\text{-}TCr = -0.01947\ X^3 + 3.45916\ X^2 - 86.2879\ X + 71.5836 = 0$$

Roots of the equation (*i.e.*, values of X) are

= 0.859029, 28.94576, 147.861357

II TR – TCs = 0

$$TR = 625.7965 + 47.31392\ X + 1.762960\ X^2 - 0.01029\ X^3$$

$$TCs = 555.7823 + 152.9501\ X - 1.68779\ X^2 + 0.009058\ X^3$$

$$TR\text{-}TCs = -0.019348\ X^3 + 3.45075\ X^2 - 105.63618\ X + 70.0142 = 0$$

Roots of the equation (*i.e.*, values of X) are

= 0.677733, 38.313431, 139.3606038.

We reject the fractional values as economically not meaningful. With Cost Cr the goats and sheep keepers can operate the flock/herd size ranging from 28 to 147 animals. At the critical minimum flock/herd size of 28 animals, the total cost is equal to total returns. Below this size total returns are less than total cost and it is uneconomical to maintain the flock/herd size below 28 animals. Above the Critical minimum size and up to the flock/herd size of 147 animals, total returns are more than the total cost. Beyond the flock/herd size of 147 animals total cost will be more than the total returns. The operator has to perform with in the range of 28 to 147 animals to get positive returns based on total costs (TCr).

Similarly, including social cost (Cost Cs) the sheep and goats activity can be operated with the flock/herd size ranging from 38 to 139 animals. At the critical minimum flock/herd size of 38 animals the total cost is equal to total returns where the operator makes neither loss nor any profit. With the flock/herd size of less than 38 animals the operator's total cost is more than the total returns and it is uneconomical. Between the critical minimum flock/herd size and the maximum size of 139 animals total returns are more than the total cost. Beyond the flock/herd size of 139 animals total cost will be more than total returns. The operator has to perform within the range of 38 to 139 animals to get positive returns based on total cost (Cost Cs). It may be added here that this result is from the point of an individual herd keeper; including the imputed cost of grazing. However, the above result does not say anything about how many small ruminants can be maintained on a common land. Evidently, if all increase their herd/flock size, the result is not an optimum but could be away from it.

In order to identify the flock/herd size at which the net returns are optimum the marginal returns and marginal cost are worked out:

Equation I $MR - MCr = 0$

$$TR = 625.7965 + 47.31392\ X + 1.762960\ X^2 - 0.01029\ X^3$$

$$MR = \frac{d(TR)}{dx} = 47.31392 + 3.52592\ X - 0.03087\ X^2$$

$$TCr = 554.2129 + 133.6019\ X - 1.69620\ X^2 + 0.009180\ X^3$$

$$MC = \frac{d(TCr)}{dx} = 133.6019 - 3.3924\ X + 0.02754\ X^2$$

equalising MR = MC for optimal level of returns *i.e.* MR - MC = 0

$$= 47.31392 - 133.6019 + 3.52592\ X + 3.3924\ X - 0.03087\ X^2 - 0.02754\ X^2 = 0$$

$= -0.05841\,X^2 + 6.91832\,X - 86.2879 = 0$

$= 0.05841\,X^2 - 6.91832\,X + 86.2879 = 0$

Roots of the equation

$$= \frac{-b \pm \sqrt{b^2 - 4ac}}{2a}$$

$$= \frac{6.91832 \pm \sqrt{(6.91832)^2 - 4(0.05841)(86.2879)}}{2(0.05841)}$$

$$= \frac{6.91832 \pm \sqrt{47.86315 - 20.16030}}{0.11682}$$

$$= \frac{6.91832 \pm 5.26334}{0.11682}$$

$$= \frac{12.181166}{0.11682} \text{ and } \frac{1.65498}{0.11682}$$

$= 104.27$ and 14.16

Sufficient Condition:

If $\frac{d^2(Tr - TCr)}{dx^2}$ = negative, then we obtain the maximum

If $\frac{d^2(TR - TCr)}{dx^2}$ = positive, then we obtain the minimum.

To get the optimum returns, the second derivative has to be negative and we get it at the flock/herd size of 104 animals.

Equation II MR - MCs = 0

$TR = 625.7965 + 47.31392\,X + 1.762960\,X^2 - 0.01029\,X^3$

$$MR = \frac{d(TR)}{dx} = 47.31392 + 3.52592\,X - 0.03087\,X^2$$

$TCs = 555.7823 + 152.9501\,X - 1.68779\,X^2 + 0.009058\,X^3$

$$MC = \frac{d(TCs)}{dx} = 152.9501 - 3.37558\,X + 0.027174\,X^2$$

Equalising MR = MC for optimal level of returns

MR - MC = 0

$= 47.31392 - 152.9501 + 3.52592\,X + 3.37558\,X - 0.03087\,X^2 - 0.027174\,X^2 = 0$

$= 0.058044\,X^2 + 6.9015\,X - 105.63618 = 0$

$= 0.058044\,X^2 - 6.9015\,X + 105.63618 = 0$

$$\text{Roots of the equation} = \frac{-b \pm \sqrt{b^2 - 4ac}}{2a}$$

$$= \frac{6.9015 \pm \sqrt{(6.9015)^2 - 4(0.058044((105.63618)}}{2(0.058044)}$$

$$= \frac{6.9015 \pm \sqrt{47.63070 - 24.52618}}{0.11608}$$

$$= \frac{6.9015 \pm 4.80671}{0.11608}$$

$$= \frac{11.70821}{0.11608} \text{ and } \frac{2.09479}{0.11608}$$

= 100.86 and 18.04

Sufficient Condition:

If $\frac{d^2(TR - TCs)}{dx^2}$ = negative, we obtain the maximum.

If $\frac{d^2(TR - TCs)}{dx^2}$ = positive, we obtain the minimum.

To get the optimum returns, the second derivative has to be negative and we get it at the flock/herd size of 101 animals.

Equation III

MR - MCBr = 0

MR = MCBr

= 47.31392 + 3.52592 X - 0.03087X^2 = 31.07860

= -0.03087 X^2 + 3.52592X + 16.23532 = 0

$$\text{Roots of the equation} = \frac{-b \pm \sqrt{b^2 - 4ac}}{2a}$$

$$= \frac{-3.52592 \pm \sqrt{12.43211 - 4(-0.03087)(16.23532)}}{2(-0.03087)}$$

$$= \frac{-3.52592 \pm \sqrt{12.43211 - 2.00474}}{-0.06174}$$

$$= \frac{-3.52592 \pm 3.79959}{-0.06174}$$

$$= \frac{-0.27367}{0.06174} \text{ and } \frac{7.32551}{0.06174}$$

= -4.43 and 118.65

By equating marginal returns with marginal cost for optimal level of returns *i.e.* MR - MC = 0, we found that taking into account all costs including the social cost (cost Cs) the optimum level of returns are achieved when the flock/herd size constitute 101 animals where MC curve intersects with the MR curve from below. Beyond this point marginal cost begins to be more than the marginal revenue. Further, at the intersection point 'B' in figure 1 where the marginal revenue is equal to marginal cost (at the flock/herd size of 18) the loss is maximum, and the sufficient condition for optimum is not met here (see Fig-5.1 below). On cost Cs the operator is at the maximum loss when the flock/herd size constitute 18 animals. Beyond this he minimises the loss upto the flock/herd size of 39 animals, where the returns are equal to costs, and which could be the viable size for him. But the operator gets the optimum returns only when the flock/herd size constitute 101 animals. Beyond 101 animals and upto the flock/herd size of 139, the returns are positive but in a declining way. Beyond the flock/herd size of 139 it becomes an uneconomical proposition.

On cost Cr (TCr in our earlier equation) the optimum level of returns are achieved when the flock/herd size constitute 104 animals where the marginal cost curve intersects with the marginal revenue curve from below. At point 'D' in figure 1 the operator is at the optimum level of returns beyond which marginal cost will be more than the marginal returns. At the flock/herd size constituting 14 animals where the added (marginal) returns are equal to added (marginal) cost (point A in figure 1) and the loss is maximum. The sufficient condition for optimum is not met here. It could be noticed that based on cost Cr the operator is at the maximum loss when the flock/herd size constitute 14 animals. Beyond this he minimises the loss upto the flock/herd size of 29 animals, where the returns are equal to costs, and which could be the viable size for him. But the operator gets the optimum returns only when the flock/herd size constitute 104 animals. Beyond 104 animals and upto the flock/herd size of 147, the returns are positive but in a declining way. Beyond the flock/herd size of 147 it becomes an uneconomical proposition. The variation in flock/herd size in terms of optimum returns based on two types of costs is not much, being 101 animals on cost Cs and 104 based on cost Cr.

On cost Br, *i.e.*, all paid out costs (Cash & Kind), imputed value of own fodder used, interest on capital (small ruminants) and the risk premium, but excluding the imputed cost of own labour used and the imputed cost of free grazing on CPRs, the optimum level of returns are achieved when the flock/herd size constitute 119 animals where MC and MR curves intersect each other (point 'E' in figure 1). Beyond this point marginal cost begins to be more than the marginal returns. It could also be noticed here that on cost Br, the operator gets

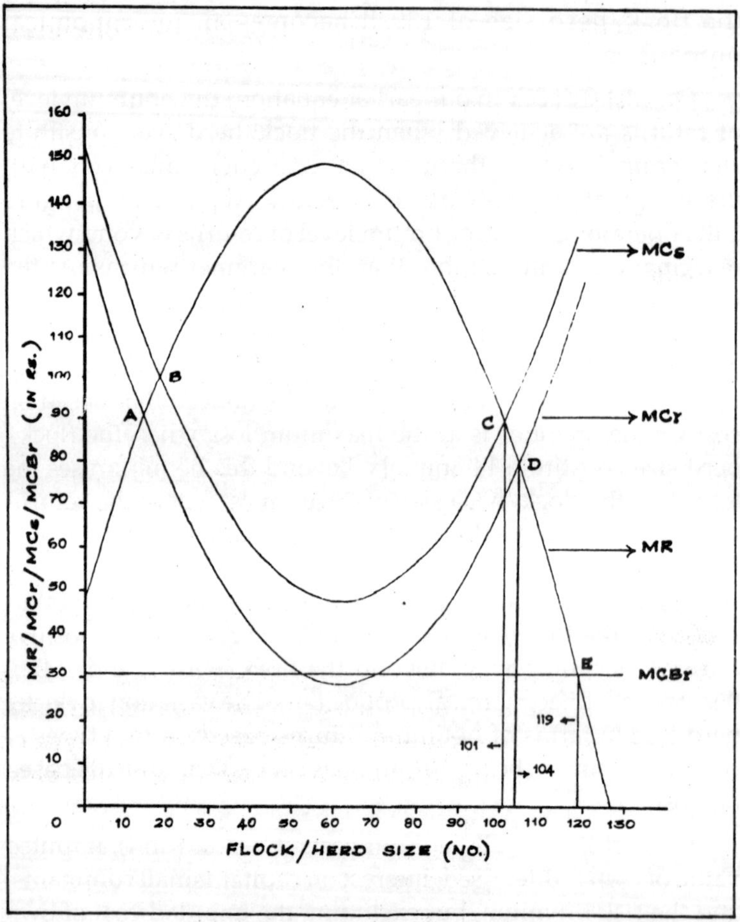
MR/MCr/MCs/MCBr (IN Rs.)
FLOCK/HERD SIZE (NO.)
MCs
MCr
MR
MCBr
A
B
C
D
E
101
104
119
0
10
20
30
40
50
60
70
80
90
100
110
120
130
140
150
160

Fig 1

the positive net returns even at one animal. That is to say, including all costs except the imputed cost of own labour and fodder from CPRs, maintaining even one animal becomes viable economically. But from our analysis we cannot say anything about the maximum size of flock/herd, beyond which the total returns are less than the total cost TCBr. In other words we cannot say anything about the range of positive net returns over TCBr. Though, returns from small ruminants over the most comprehensive concept of costs are not encouraging, rural households maintain these animals as long as they get free/cheap inputs like fodder and labour. Whatever they get as returns minus of paid out costs are substantial for them. In relative terms even the marginal returns are much more, particularly to the poor and landless. Small ruminants are maintained by them even at marginal returns as an hedge against risk and uncertainty and as part of their comprehensive survival strategy. Returns could have been much more if good quality breeds are maintained along with sustainable use of grazing lands and other CPRs.

5.9 Characteristics of Efficient Households Vis-a-Vis Inefficient Households in Keeping Small Ruminants

We have also tried to distinguish between the most efficient and the least efficient households in terms of their socio-economic characteristics. Evidently, hardly a few have economically optimum size of herd. The households keeping small ruminants, can however, be arranged in order of efficiency as reflected in output-input ratios. On the output side we have taken the gross returns in rupees. Input side constitute all paid out cost, value of own fodder used, rent paid on share cropping, imputed cost of own labour and cost on account of risk premium (all in rupees). We have not taken into account the imputed cost of free grazing by goats and sheep in this analysis.

After arranging all the households with small ruminants in descending order of output-input ratios (as explained above), 25 per cent of the households from above were identified as most efficient households and the other 25 per cent at the bottom as least efficient households. To have a comparison across the two groups some of their important characteristics identified are:

1. Type of households (rich, poor or landless),
2. Land holding size and the extent of land under irrigation,
3. Total size of livestock holding,
4. Size of small ruminants holding,
5. Whether operating largely on own labour or hired labour,
6. Whether owners or lessees of small ruminants on 'share cropping' basis.

The total number of households with small ruminants being 102, we have 25 households in the category of most efficient and 25 households in the category of the least efficient (25 per cent in each category). Among the 25 most efficient, 8 were rich, 16 were poor peasants and one was a landless labour household. Among 25 least efficient, 2 were rich, 23 were poor peasants and there was none from the landless labour class. Though the poor peasants dominate in both the categories, this is because of their numerical dominance in the total sample also. To see where they relatively dominate, we have taken the proportion of each class (rich/poor peasant) in each category (most/least efficient) under Item 1 in Table 5.16. Thus, 21.6 per cent of rich peasants are in the most efficient category but only 5.4 per cent of them in the least efficient. This suggests their relative dominance in the most efficient, but not their concentration. This is because even in the most efficient, their proportion is less than 25 per cent which is the proportion of all households in the category. In contrast, 26.2 per cent of the poor peasants are in the most efficient but 37.7 per cent of them are in the least efficient. This suggests the relative dominance of the poor peasants among the least efficient. Surprisingly, of the four landless labour households one is in the most efficient category, and none in the least efficient. In terms of concentration, while the rich peasants as well as the landless are concentrated among the middle 50 per cent (neither most nor least efficient), the poor are relatively more concentrated among the least efficient.

Table 5.16

Efficient Vis-a-Vis Inefficient Households in Keeping Small Ruminants

Characteristics	*Most efficient house-holds*	*Least efficient house-holds*
1. *(a)* Percentage of rich peasants in the category to total number rich peasants	21.6	5.4
(b) Percentage of poor peasants in the category to total number poor peasants	26.2	37.7
(c) Percentage of landless labour households in the category to total number landless labour households	25.0	-
2. *(a)* Average size of land holding per household (acres)	4.27	2.11
(b) Percentage of land under irrigation	7.7	5.2
3. *(a)* Average size of livestock holding per household	28	18
(b) Average size of small ruminant holding per household	16	10
4. *(a)* Proportion of households operating small ruminants on own labour as percent of total households in the most/least efficient category respectively	12	92
(b) Proportion of households operating small ruminants on hired-in labour as percent of total households in the most/least efficient category respectively	88	8
5. *(a)* Percentage of household owning small ruminants	100	80
(b) Percentage of household operating small ruminants on 'share cropping' basis	-	20

Most efficient households operate on an average a flock/ herd size of 16 goats and sheep per household as compared with least efficient households who hold on average 10 small ruminants. Apart from owning large size of land holdings (4.27 acres as compared with 2.11 acres in the case of least efficient households), the most efficient households also operate larger areas of irrigated lands. Further, the most efficient group owns small ruminants as compared with the least efficient households who are also share croppers. Most efficient group operate their animals largely on hired labour as compared with the least efficient group. On the other hand, the least efficient group uses more of own labour. Further, the least efficient have less waiting power and tend to sell animals when quite young, *i.e.,* before full productive potential is used (as seen from table 5.8, the organic increase is a smaller proportion of gross income in their case).

6

ECONOMICS OF SHEEP VIS-A-VIS GOATS

6.1 Holdings of Sheep *Vis-a-Vis* Goats Across Class of Rural Households

Goats belong to the genus *Capra*; sheep to the genus, *Ovis*. Within small ruminants goats are much more hardy than sheep and adapt themselves to any type of situation. The preferred browsing habit of goats is especially advantageous under dry range conditions in which the surviving vegetation tends to be on deep rooted shrubs and bushes. Though goats are basically browsers, they also adapt themselves to grazing whenever required. Nevertheless sheep and goats could be considered as supplementary to each other within a certain level of grazing intensity because of the different varieties of vegetation they consume. However, they are competitive as they compete for the same capital and labour at the household level.

Goats are more agile and thus are able to feed over much rougher terrain than sheep. This agility combined with an ability to travel further without water can greatly increase their feeding range than in the case of sheep. But in an eco-system where the vegetation constitute largely grass than shrubs and bushes keeping sheep could be much more advantageous. In fact the browsing behavior of goats reduces their exposure to endoparasites but, when heavily stocked on grass, goats seem more prone to heavy infestation than sheep. Diseases which appear to affect goats more than sheep include

Caprine Arthritis Encephalitis (CAE) and Brucellosis (Thedford, 1983 a, b as quoted in Winrock International, 1983).

Goats are much more prolific than sheep. The goat kid once a year. Kidding 3 times in two years is not un-common. Giving birth to twins is common among goats. Many goat keepers have also reported of 3 kids per pregnancy among goats. Though the sheep lamb once in a year, twins among them are uncommon. The sex ratio at birth among both sheep and goats is 50 : 50, and the gestation period being of five months duration. Though both sheep and goats are meat animals, they differ in terms of their by-products. Sheep yield wool as its by-product whereas goats yield milk. While grazing, sheep can be easily managed by women, children and aged, whereas goats require generally young and strong persons to manage their grazing browsing.

Generally it is believed that goats are maintained by the poor and landless whereas sheep by all types of households. In our study villages it was found that over 75 per cent of both rich and poor peasants respectively have maintained goats. However, while 54 per cent of rich peasants kept sheep, only 31 per cent of the poor peasants kept them. None of the landless kept sheep (see Table 6.1). Thus our data shows that sheep are relatively preferred more by the rich who have more land than the poor, whereas the poor have a greater preference for goats. This also proves our earlier statement elsewhere that some amount of own land goes in favor of keeping sheep rather than goats. This is because, stubbles and grass from the bunds of own land supplements the fodder requirements of sheep to some extent. It was reported by poor peasants and the landless that in the recent past they too had maintained more sheep than at present along with the goats. But the shortage of grass and other herbages from pastures, tank beds and tank foreshores has forced them to concentrate more on goats which could be maintained on hill slopes, gravelly lands, road sides, scrub forests etc. than on the sheep.

Table 6.1

Average Flock / Herd Size and Number of Households Keeping Sheep *Vis-a-vis* Goats Across Class of Rural Households

	Total No. of hhs with small ruminants	*Sheep*		*Goats*		*Proportion (%) among small ruminants of*	
		No. of hhs. maintaining sheep	*Average flock size per hh*	*No. of hhs. maintaining sheep*	*Average flock size per hh*	*Sheep*	*Goats*
Rich Peasants	37	20 (54.1)	28	28 (75.7)	25	44.2	55.8
Poor Peasants	61	19 (31.1)	12	46 (75.4)	14	25.4	74.6
Landless Labour	4	-	-	4 (100)	14	-	100.0
All	102	39 (38.2)	20	78 (76.5)	18	35.6	64.4

Note : Figures in the brackets are percentages to the respective totals in the rows. Since many households have maintained both sheep and goats, their break-up overlaps. The average size is per household possessing sheep/goats respectively, and not the average taking into account total number of households in each class.

Among small ruminants, goats were numerically more dominant accounting for over 64 per cent, with sheep accounting for less than 36 per cent. The proportion of goats was even higher, being 75 per cent among the poor peasants and 100 per cent among the landless, compared to 56 per cent among the rich. Even the rich preferred to keep more goats than sheep, but this preference was stronger among the poor (see Table 6.1).

Further, though a larger proportion of rich as well as poor peasants have maintained goats than sheep, the average flock and herd size of holdings are more or less the same. In the case of rich peasants, the average size of sheep *vis-a-vis* goats holding is 28 and 25 animals respectively, whereas it was 12 sheep and 14 goats among the poor peasants (Table 6.1). This shows that there is no variation across goats and sheep as far as the size of holding is concerned. But one can notice the variation in size of sheep *vis-a-vis* goats holding across class of rural households. Rich peasants are able to manage a bigger size irrespective of goats or sheep as compared with the poor peasants. This could be, apart from other reasons like availability of capital and fodder, because of the housing condition. Rich peasants generally possess bigger houses and in many cases a separate house/shed for livestock, and hence manage a larger flock/herd size of sheep and goats. On the other hand, poor peasants and landless labour households keep their animals during nights mostly in their small dwelling houses (in many cases a small hut) and hence could not maintain larger flock/herd sizes.

6.2 Relative Contribution of Sheep Vis-a-Vis Goats Among Small Ruminants to Gross Returns

The share of gross returns from goats to total returns from small ruminants was higher (being 70.1 per cent) than from sheep, being only 29.9 per cent (Table 6.2). Across class of rural households, contribution of goats to total income from small ruminants is much higher in the case of poor peasants and landless labour households than in the case of rich peasants. The landless labour households have maintained only goats and no sheep. Even in the case of rich peasants share of goats to total income from small ruminants is substantial, being 62.6 per cent than from sheep. This shows that goats play relatively an important rôle in the economy of rural households, particularly more so in the economy of poor peasants and landless labour households. Another interesting aspect of the contribution of goats to gross returns is that it is higher than its numerical share. This was so not only for all households taken together, but also in the case of rich peasants and poor peasants alike. Nevertheless, contribution of sheep is also important in the economy of rich and poor peasants. Among small ruminants, both goats and sheep are mainly meat animals, *i.e.*, neither the goats are milch animals nor the sheep yield substantial wool. Returns from goats are higher than from sheep, mainly because goats are more prolific, less susceptible to disease, and are hardy.

Table 6.2

Share (Per cent) of Gross Returns from Goats *Vis-a-Vis* Sheep to Total Gross Returns from Small Ruminants

	Share (Per cent) from		
	Goats	*Sheep*	*Small Ruminants*
Rich Peasants	62.6	37.4	100
Poor Peasants	79.5	20.5	100
Landless Labour	100	-	100
All	70.1	29.9	100

6.3 Gross Returns from Sheep *Vis-a-Vis* Goats and Their Composition

The major component of gross returns from sheep is the sale of animals, whereas it is the organic increase in the case of goats. It can be seen from Table 6.3 that the share on account of animals sold constitute around 50 per cent of the gross returns from sheep per household, whereas it is much less from goats, being 27.4 per cent. The share of organic increase, which is an addition to the stock, is much more in the case of goats (64.1 per cent) than sheep (26.4 per cent). This also shows that though the peasants sell both goats and sheep regularly, the stock of goats is affected much less than the stock of sheep, since the rate of organic increase is much more in the case of former than later. The higher rate of organic increase among goats also helps the peasants to build the stock particularly after the drought. On the other hand the lower organic increase among sheep could be an advantage where there is scarcity of fodder.

Table 6.3

Different Components of Gross Returns from Sheep *Vis-a-Vis* Goats

(Rs. Per Household)

	Sheep	*Goats*
1. Net change in the value of stock (mainly organic increase)	536 (26.4)	1524 (64.1)
2. Sale of animals	1005 (49.4)	651 (27.4)
3. Manure	185 (9.1)	173 (7.3)
4. Wool	2 (0.1)	–
5. Milk	-	0.3 (0.01)
6. Skin	28 (1.4)	3 (0.1)
7. Income from dead animals	277 (13.6)	26 (1.1)
8. Total Returns	2033 (100)	2377 (100)

Note : Figures in the brackets are percentages.

More than 9 per cent and around 8 per cent of the gross returns constitute the share of manure (droppings collected) from sheep and goats respectively. Though there is no regular practice of sheep folding in the study region, the droppings of sheep while grazing stubbles are valued very much as rich organic manure. The contribution of wool to total returns from sheep per household is negligible, being 0.1 per cent. Wool produced by the local sheep is rough and coarse which is used in the manufacturing of rough blankets. Income from such wool is not important to the sheep producers. Generally, shearing of sheep is done once in a year and quite a few sheep keepers shear them once in two years. The average yield of wool per shearing of an adult animal ranges from 250 to 500 grams. Further, goats are hardly milked for sale. The imputed value of milk used for own consumption is also negligible, being 0.01 per cent of the gross returns from goats. The other important source of income from sheep is the returns realised from the sale of dead animals. Its share accounts around 14 per cent of the gross returns, which also reflects the level of mortality among sheep in the study region. In fact as the share of such returns increases, actual income from sheep declines. Unlike from sheep, returns realised from the sale of dead animals is negligible (1.1 per cent) in goat production. This shows that the level of mortality among goats is much less as compared with sheep (see Table 7.3). This also supports our earlier statement elsewhere that goats are hardy and less risky than sheep, and hence many households particularly the poor and landless prefer to maintain goats than sheep. This could also be one of the main reasons, apart from prolificacy, which favor a higher growth rate among goats than sheep even at the macro level.

6.4 Net Returns from Sheep *Vis-a-Vis* Goats as Per Different Cost Concepts

The important costs involved in sheep *vis-a-vis* goat production are the cost of labour and fodder. In the case of households who have maintained both sheep as well as goats together and same amount of labour is used for both, we have apportioned the total labour cost between goats and sheep as per the flock/herd size. Table 6.4 shows that 57.1 per cent and 16.5 per cent of the total costs in sheep production are accounted for by imputed cost of own labour and imputed cost of grazing on CPRs respectively. In the case of goat production, the imputed cost of own labour is slightly higher (62.8 per cent) than in the case of sheep, whereas imputed cost of grazing on CPRs constitutes 13.5 per cent of the total costs. Further, the paid out cost including the wages paid to hired-in labour is marginal both in sheep as well as goat production, being 3.2 and 2.3 per cent respectively. Though there is the system of leasing-in and leasing-out of sheep in other parts of Karnataka[9], no such system is in operation in the study villages. Hence, there is no rent paid on account of 'share cropping' by the households in the case of sheep, though this practice is prevalent in the case of goats. A few households among the rich as well as poor peasants have leased-in the goats and paid the rent, which constitute 1.2 per cent of the total cost. The system of leasing-in of goats was more common among the poor and landless. But now it is the rich and poor peasants who have leased-in the goats, whereas no such cases reported among the landless labour households. As per the 'share-cropping' system, goats are leased-out for a period of about 2 to 3 years. First year's kid goes to the lessee. Second or third year's kids along with the mother will go to the lessor. If the doe kid twins, the owner will get the female kid and the lessee will retain the male kid. Generally the common share cropping system is followed by all the rural households, though there is scope for flexibility as far as the contract between the

9. Even in the study villages taking sheep in lease, particularly by the poor and landless from the rich households was in operation till the recent past. Adult ewes were leased in for a period of 2 to 3 years and the owner gets back his animals along with 2nd or 3rd years' lambs at the end of the contract period. One who maintains the sheep on lease will retain the 1st or 2nd year's lamb. This was one among the traditional institutional arrangements in the villages which helped many poor and landless to build their own stock of sheep. But due to the degradation and shrinkage of CPRs maintaining leased in sheep has become difficult for the poor and landless.

lesser and the lessee is concerned. The bulk of the lessees were from the poor peasants. There were, however, a few lessees from rich peasant class as well. No landless labourer either leased-in or leased out small ruminants.

Table 6.4

Composition of Costs in the Rearing of Sheep Vis-a-Vis Goats

(Rs. Per Household)

	Sheep	*Goats*
1. Paid out cost (cash and kind)	77 (3.2)	58 (2.3)
2. Rent paid on leased-in animals	-	32 (1.2)
3. Imputed interest on capital (livestock)	434 (17.9)	403 (15.7)
4. Imputed cost of own labour used	1387 (57.1)	1608 (62.6)
5. Risk premium	130 (5.3)	122 (4.7)
6. Imputed cost of grazing in CPRs	401 (16.5)	347 (13.5)
7. Total cost	2429 (100)	2570 (100)

Note : Figures in the brackets are percentages to total.

As far as the costs are concerned, the difference between sheep and goats arise mainly in terms of cost C1. In other words more own labour is used both per animal as well as per household in the rearing of goats than sheep. Whereas, the paid out costs per animal are same in both the cases (Table 6.5). The relative economics of sheep *vis-a-vis* goats can be examined by looking at the table 6.6. Though the net returns from sheep *vis-a-vis* goats are negative (over total costs Cs), they are much less from goats than sheep. The net returns are positive over all other costs and are much more in goat

Table 6.5

Costs and Gross Returns (Rs.) from Sheep *Vis-a-Vis* Goats Per Year

		Costs							*Gross Returns*
		A1	*A2*	*B1*	*Br*	*C1*	*Cr*	*Cs*	
Sheep	Per household	76	76	510	640	1898	2097	2429	2033
	Per animal	3	3	25	31	94	101	121	101
Goats	Per household	57	89	492	615	2100	2223	2570	2377
	Per animal	3	4	27	33	115	122	141	131

Table 6.6

Net Returns (Rs.) from Sheep *Vis-a-Vis* Goats Using Different Cost Concepts

		Costs						
		A1	*A2*	*B1*	*Br*	*C1*	*Cr*	*Cs*
Sheep	Per household	1957	1957	1523	1393	135	6	-396
	Per animal	98	98	76	70	7	0	-20
Goats	Per household	2320	2288	1885	1762	277	154	-193
	Per animal	128	127	104	98	16	9	-10

production than in sheep. More than this, over cost C1 (as cost C1 is more in the case of goats than sheep) net returns from goats both per household as well as per animal are substantial, being Rs. 277 and Rs. 16 respectively as compared with sheep, being only Rs. 135 and Rs. 7 per household and per animal in their case respectively. This also shows that though more own labour is used in goat production, it pays for it. That could be one of the reasons why many rural households, particularly the poor and landless with greater availability of own labour, with its zero or negligible opportunity costs, prefer to have goats in their household economies. In fact this could be one of the strongest reasons which favoured higher number of goats than sheep, in spite of the ban on the former than the later in many places.

7

MARKETING OF SMALL RUMINANTS AND THEIR BY-PRODUCTS

7.1 Role of Markets in Small Ruminants Activity

A good marketing system of agricultural commodities will help in increasing the level of agricultural production apart and promote rural welfare. The role of markets or trade would depend on the nature and type of functionaries involved. If the marketing and related services are provided by monopsonistic elements, peasants can become easy victims of exploitation.

The economics of small ruminants too depends on sound marketing system for goats and sheep and their by-products. About 14.8 million sheep and 35 million goats are slaughtered annually in the organised slaughter houses in India (Bhasin, 1988). In the study villages, though the level of meat consumption was reported to have slightly increased, the demand for meat in the form of sheep and goats on hoofs has declined. In other words the marketable goats and sheep are sold out to urban centres, and the villagers/consumers purchase the required quantity of meat at a higher price from the urban markets. Within the village or across the selected three villages, not even a single sheep or goat was purchased by the rural households for own consumption during the reference period. Only two households belonging to the rich peasant class slaughtered one animal each during the reference year from their own stock for own consumption; one because of its disease and the other for the annual festival, 'Jathre Habba'. There is a system of purchasing a sheep or goat annually during the time of festival by a group of households within the village and sharing the meat among themselves. But otherwise those who are better off and afford to buy the sheep or goat meat, buy it from the neighbouring towns.

The increased demand for small ruminants is not from the rural households but from the increasing urban population. The increased income as a result of increasing demand for sheep and goats from the urban population has helped the rural households to meet their other household requirements from the sale of small ruminants. Once or twice in a year during the time of festivals, when demand for meat shoots up, the urban traders along with local traders and middlemen become very active in the trade of sheep and goats. The producers of small ruminants in general have a high bargaining power in their transactions only during such periods. Prices are fixed based on the supply of animals. The excess demand during festivals raises the prices of the animals. The benefits of the rise in the price of live animals during the peak periods do reach the producers in terms of higher price, but the traders, middlemen and the retailers also gain through increased turnover in spite of a lower margin. During the normal season the demand for sheep and goats normally remains constant, and the traders keep their margin of profit high. Though there is a spurt in the sale of sheep and goats during the peak (festival) season, a larger number of animals are sold during the normal season of the year since the peak season demand for animals last only a couple of days. An increased supply of goats and sheep tends to lead to a crash in the price of animals affecting the small ruminant keepers very much, but prices of meat do not fall. Traders and middlemen earn more per animal during the normal seasons than during peak seasons. It is the poor and landless sheep and goats keepers who are hit hard during the normal season, that is the major part of the year and the traders have a high bargaining power.

If we estimate the value of a live animal taking into account the average retail price of sheep or goat meat and the skin during a year, less than half of the estimated value goes to the producers (sheep and goats raisers). More than half of the total returns are shared by the middlemen, trader and the retailer (butcher). In other words, not even 50 per cent of the consumer price goes to the keepers of goats and sheep. Despite increases in the retail price of meat, proportionate benefits have not reached the primary producers to provide incentive for more meat production (NCA, 1976).

The average price of an animal on hoof (with an average live weight of about 25 kgs) recorded in the sample villages was Rs. 300 to 400 during the study period. We have also recorded the average retail price of mutton and goat meat at Rs. 50 per kg. This was based on the retail price in Bagepalli town, Kolar town and Bangalore city. We have taken the average of Bagepalli, Kolar and Bangalore, since a large number of animals from the study region are slaughtered in these urban centers though animals are also transported from these centers to far off places in Andhra Pradesh and other parts of Karnataka. We have taken the average retail price of mutton and goat meat during one year, since there is not much variation in the price of mutton and goat meat across seasons in a year. However, an increasing trend in the price of mutton and goat meat takes place through spurts in prices once in a year or two. After dressing the animal weighing about 25 Kgs. the butcher can get on an average net mutton/meat of about 15 kgs. At the rate of Rs. 40 per kg. total returns from meat/ mutton sold could be Rs. 600 per animal. The value of offals, stomach, head etc. could be around Rs. 100. The skin is valued at an average price of Rs. 100 per piece. Thus, the total retail sale value of an animal could be Rs. 800. What the producers (sheep/goats raiser) get is less than half (Rs. 300 to 400 per animal) of the total proceeds from the sale of an animal. Roughly 10 per cent of the surplus (about Rs. 50) goes to the broker/middleman and the remaining to the trader/retailer cum butcher. As we have mentioned earlier, sheep and goats are slaughtered regularly due to stable demand irrespective of any season in the urban centers. Traders, middlemen and the retailers remain active the whole year to buy sheep and goats at reasonably lower prices.

7.2 Marketing Structure of Goats and Sheep in the Study Region

A sound marketing structure increases the value of a commodity as it passes from one stage of processing and location to the other commensurate with the cost of processing and services involved. A good market structure also improves the access of the direct producer to the market and ensures him good value for the commodity sold by him. Often, however, too many agents come in between the producers and consumers than required, and tend to exploit both the producers as well as the consumers. Consumers may have to pay more to buy the commodity and the producers may not get proper share in the consumer's rupee. From this perspective, we shall try to understand the nature of the marketing structure in the case of small ruminants.

In the marketing of goats and sheep many agents/traders come in between till the animals are sold to the final consumers. Chart I shows that in the study region goats and sheep produced in the villages pass through many channels till they reach the urban consumers. Some of these channels are direct to the consumer, but some are through more than one or two intermediaries. The direct channel is used only rarely and when used, mostly by rich peasants. Formal marketing of these animals take place at any time any day within the village.

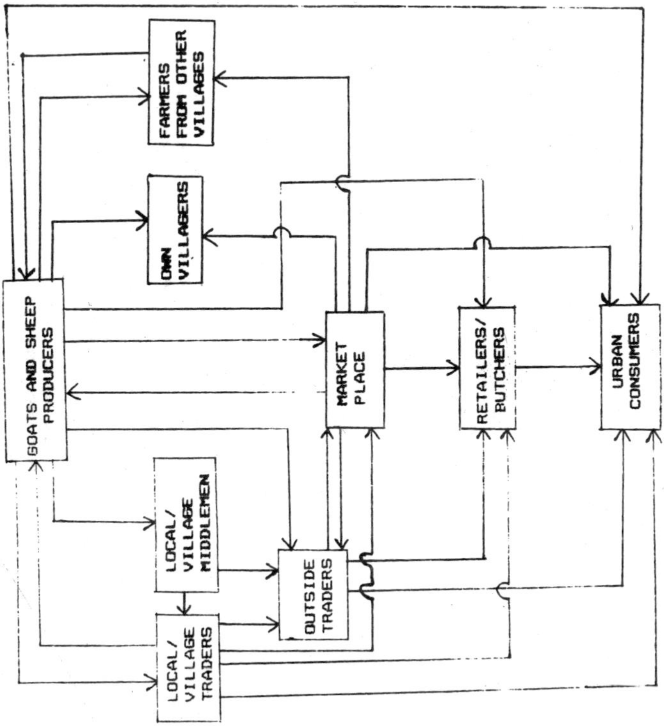

Chart 7.1

Marketing Structure of Boats and Sheep in the Study Region

The local traders purchase sheep and goats both from the producers as well as from the village middlemen, and then sell in the market place or to retailers/butchers. The local traders act also as the hoarders of sheep and goats. Whenever producers particularly the poor and landless, are badly in need of money, the local traders bargain with them and purchase the animals at a lower rate. They keep the animals in their houses until they find a person from urban areas for whom they can sell the animals at a higher margin. The hoarded animals are also sold at the market place/shandies to the urban retailers/butchers and consumers. Depending on the bargain they make with villagers, they buy upto even ten animals at a time. They often pool the purchased animals over a period of one weak or a month and sell them in the regular shandies/ market place. Local middlemen work for the local traders though occasionally they too buy one or more animals on their own and sell them to any one they like. The difference between the local traders (Kuri meke vyapari) and local middlemen (Kuri meke Dallali) is that the former are actual buyers whereas the later largely act as brokers between the producers and the local traders. The middlemen get commission from the local traders for their services and some times from both the traders as well as the producers. The local traders are the most active agents among the sheep and goats traders in the study villages. They are often the kith and kins of the producers, which also help them to a certain extent to have a upper hand in this trade.

Apart from local traders and middlemen who purchase animals from peasants, outside traders also come to the villages and purchase. Several peasants—both rich as also the poor—have direct links with outside traders, but their sales also often take place locally. Such access to outsiders creates some degree of competition from which mainly the rich peasants seem to benefit. Having more animals to offer, the traders go to them more and strike a bargain. The poor peasants on the other

Table 7.1

Number of Goats and Sheep Raisers who have Marketed their Animals to Different Marketing Agents During the Study Period

Category of Households	*No. of Households*	*Local Traders/ Muddlemen at the Village*	*Sale to Outside Traders at the Villages*	*Sold at the Market Place/Shandy**	*Rural Families*	*No Sales*
Rich Peasants	37	20	15	3	4	2
		(541)	(40.5)	(8.1)	(10.8)	(5.4)
Poor Peasants	61	26	29	-	2	12
		(42.6)	(47.5)		(3.3)	(9.7)
Landless Labour	4	4	-	-	-	-
		(100)				
All	102	50	44	3	6	14
		(49.0)	(43.1)	(2.9)	(5.9)	(13.7)

* Market place/shandy is around 20kms from the study villages.

Note : Figures in the brackets are percentages to total households in the respective rows. Since many households sell their animals to more than one buyer their total overlaps.

hand and the landless have less bargaining power, as the number of animals they can offer for sale is far too limited to create sufficient interest for viable sale.

It can be seen from Table 7.1 that 49 per cent of the producers have sold their animals to local traders and middlemen of the village, and another 43 per cent sell to outside traders at the villages. Only 3 per cent of the peasants, all of them from the richer peasantry, took their animals outside for sale. All landless households sold their animals locally. The direct sale to rural households within the villages was reported by only 6 per cent of families—both from rich and poor peasants.

Since there are many agents in the trade of goats and sheep it may appear that it creates additional employment or atleast a somewhat competitive situation. But such a structure has also to support a large number of intermediaries each striving to make a living at the expense of peasants, and hence involves duplication and waste, resulting in higher prices for consumers and lower share in the price to producers. However, it cannot be denied that a multiplicity of agents does ensure some amount of competitive situation. There were no instances of peasants being tied up to the traders by credit, and the peasants were largely free to make their transactions with whomsoever they wanted.

7.3 Marketing of By-Products from Small Ruminants

By-products from small ruminants like wool and manure (droppings) are sold within the village. Manure is hardly marketed outside the village. The rich peasants never sell the manure. The poor peasants and landless exchange it either for money, fodder or grains. Though the production and yield of wool in the study region is negligible, there exists a regular market for it. The traders and weavers from other parts of Karnataka and the State of Andhra Pradesh do come regularly once in a year to shear the animals in the village. They do not take money for their services. In turn they retain the sheared wool for themselves and pay the sheep owners some nominal money based on their own judgements. Usually in many cases a coarse woollen blanket is given in exchange of wool. The sheep raisers never shear their sheep on their own nor take the wool for marketing elsewhere.

Skins, intestines and blood are the other major by-products, accounting for 14.4 percent of the total value realised from the slaughter of an animal (Seshagiri Rao, 1988). Skins are used in the manufacture of various types of leathers, which in turn are used to produce consumer products like shoes, gloves, handbags etc. Important products based on the skin of small ruminants, which are exported from India, include soft leathers, footwear uppers, fancy goods, ladies handbags, garments, gloves etc. As far as goat and sheep skins are concerned their recovery is almost complete in the study region. Skins are mobilized from villages and semi-urban areas to various markets from where they are dispatched to different tanning centers within the state as well as outside the state.

The duration between collection and processing of the skins depend on the type and length of market chain, hoarding practices, season, distance between the market place and the collection centers etc. Generally from semi-urban areas and the villages it require much longer time than in urban centers till the skins are dispatched to the tanneries. Skins procured in urban centres are transported within 2 weeks to the tanneries. From rural areas the time lag may reach 2 months. As far as the goats and sheep skins are concerned the longer the market chain, the higher is the ultimate price markup over the basic procurement price (Seshagiri Rao, 1988). The traders or middlemen engaged in the business of slaughtered skins from goats and sheep are different from those who are engaged in the trade of animals on hoof. In the trade of slaughtered skins from urban centers the role of middlemen is limited and the butcher will get a fair price, whereas the primary producers of the rural areas remain in a disadvantageous position. The price markup of small ruminants skin at the tanner's stage can reach 45% over the price originally paid to the primary producers at the village (CLRI, 1987).

Another important by-product from small ruminants is blood. Blood accounts for 3.5-5.5% of the body weight of an animal (Seshagiri Rao, 1988). Small ruminants' blood is rich in protein and iron and hence obtained from the slaughtered animal for consumption. But in the study region most of the blood is wasted due to lack of proper facilities and poor slaughterhouses. Small ruminants' blood can be collected scientifically and mixed with wheat bran or with treated "ruminal contents" (blood meal) so that it can be used as an animal feed supplement.

Most of the intestines from the slaughtered goats and sheep are consumed locally. Due to the high price of meat, there is good demand for intestines from the consumers. If properly collected and processed intestines of goats and sheep could be used in edible products and sausage casings. Intestines could also be used in the production of surgical, sports and musical guts.

Though small ruminants are very important as a source of income to the rural families, their potential has not yet been realised as a source of meat for human consumption and provide raw materials like skins, wool, hair, intestines, blood etc. to the industrial sector. Particularly the collection of by-products from small ruminants is most in-efficient, and hence a substantial loss to the economy.

7.4 Marketing Problems of the Goats and Sheep Raisers

Goats and sheep keepers face the problem of marketing of both small ruminants as well as their by-products. There is no well organised marketing system for small ruminants and their by-products in the study region. Farmers have to travel a long distance to market their animals in the weekly/monthly shandies. While travelling with the animals, as well as till the animals are sold in the shandies, they face the problem of fodder and water for their animals, as a result of which the body weight of the animals decreases and they lose substantial returns. That is one of the important reasons why many households sell their animals within the village to the traders/middlemen rather than facing the problems in the market place/shandies. The traders/middlemen, both from within the village as well as from other areas, exploit the sheep and goats keepers by fixing the rate per animal or per flock/herd on rough estimates of weight, which is generally an underestimate.

At the market place/shandies many a time brokers/middleman and traders collude among themselves and never bid/purchase the animals beyond a certain price. Often instead of bidding, one of the traders purchase the flock/herd at a fixed price and the other traders will not compete with him and later they share the animals among them. Since the sellers come from a long distance to the market place/shandies are compelled to dispose off their animals as early as possible. Usually marketing starts in the morning and it will be over by the evening of the same day. There is no regulated market yard/place for small ruminants in the study region. Nor is there any question of the state interfering in its marketing by way of support price/procurement price. In fact many small ruminants keepers are unaware of the actual value of their animals in the larger economy. In other words they are not aware of their share in the consumer's rupee realised by the total transaction of goats and sheep (including their by-products) in the larger market. If it is known, at least to a greater extent they can form their co-operatives or can take necessary precautions while selling their animals. There is no regular broadcasting through Radio/TV of the prices of goats and sheep and their by-products in different parts, as it is done in the case of other agricultural commodities. Instead of being cheated at the hands of the traders/brokers at the market place/shandies whom they do not know, and to avoid the problems like travel expenses, scarcity of fodder and water to their animals, most of the goats and sheep keepers prefer to sell their animals within their villages rather than at the market place/shandies.

Even at the village sheep and goats keepers are not free from exploitation by the traders and middlemen. Traders and middlemen from other areas approach the owners of sheep and goats either directly or through the local traders/ middlemen. Price is fixed either on per animal basis or for the total disposable flock/herd. It is fixed on crude guess or estimate rather than by actually weighing the animal. The goats and sheep raisers lose much in this system since their knowledge about rough estimate of animal weight is very poor as compared with the traders or the middlemen.

Marketing of wool in the study region is still primitive. The same age old system of bartering coarse wool for blankets still exist. The shearer-cum-trader from other areas make good profit by continuing this system. Though the sheep raisers hardly account the wool they produce, it would add much to their returns if it is properly marketed. What the producers get from the shearer-cum-trader either in the form of a *blanket* or money is negligible. It has been recorded in the study villages that on an average an adult sheep yield around 500 grams of coarse wool per annum. The producer will get hardly Rs. 0.50 to 0.75 per sheep (*i.e.* per 500 grams). If the flock is large the producer will get a coarse woollen blanket in exchange of wool sheared from 15 to 20 animals. The knowledge about the utility of wool in the larger economy is also very poor among the producers. Added to this there is no good marketing system for wool in the study region.

A good marketing system of both small ruminants as well as their by-products can increase the level of income of the goats and sheep keepers. It can also protect both the primary producers as well as the consumers from a large number of middlemen. Both goats and sheep on hoofs as well as their by-products could be efficiently procured and marketed through sound co-operative systems. With this if the infrastructure facilities like good roads, availability of water and fodder in market places, proper slaughter houses, efficient market places etc. are provided, small ruminants activity could become one of the important strategies of rural development.

8

SMALL RUMINANTS AND THE ENVIRONMENT

8.1 Overcoming Risk and Uncertainty and Adjustment to Drought by the Rural Households

In droughtprone regions rural households are subjected to risk and uncertainty, particularly during and after the drought. Often, farmers could not recover even the input costs from crop cultivation. Households had to store food grains not only for the current year's consumption but also for one more year to meet the eventuality of crop failure. But such a strategy could be available only to the rich peasants. Poor peasants and landless labour could not meet even the current year's consumption requirements.

Rural households adopt several strategies to cope with risk and uncertainty. As far as possible and with an eye on profits ago, they try to use free inputs in crop cultivation as well as in animal husbandry so as to minimise the paid out costs. Though in crop cultivation more HYV seeds and chemical fertilisers are used than own seeds and farm yard manure since the profits from the use are high, risk averse farmers shy away firm cross-bred cows which involve significant paid-out costs. Such farmers are also cautious about keeping herds of local cows so that the risk of the scarcity of fodder and water is minimised. Further, rich peasants concentrate on other non-agricultural activities as an insurance, whereas poor and landless depend on wage employment created by the government under anti-poverty and other relief programmes.

Poor peasants and landless labour also depend on non-governmental organisation (NGO) for wage employment particularly during the slack seasons. Further, borrowing at times of difficulties from relatives, friends and money lenders is also common among them.

Keeping a few local non-descript cows, goats and sheep as an hedge against risk and uncertainty is also common among the rural households. One or two local cows are maintained on CPRs for milk which can also be sold though at a lower price during drought. Goats and sheep are much more helpful for them particularly after the drought, since small ruminants withstand the stress of drought much longer than large ruminants, and they can be readily sold at any time. Even the rich peasants concentrate on goats and sheep to a greater extent since the income from crop cultivation as well as from other non-agricultural activities become uncertain during and after the occurrence of drought. It is for this reason that small ruminants are relatively more dominant as observed in chapter 5. A relative dominance of small ruminants is thus more a consequence of scarcity and uncertainty of biomass availability rather than its cause—a point which a recent committee appointed by the Government of India also emphasised (India, 1987).

8.2 Fodder Availability and Grazing Habits

In a mixed crop-livestock farming system keeping sheep and goats depend to a considerable extent on the availability of fodder from uncultivated lands and other common property resources including the forests. Arable lands too contribute to the fodder requirements of small ruminants in the form of stubble grazing but maintaining sheep and goats on such lands could be difficult. In small ruminants' diet grasses and shrups from CPRs are more important than the crop by-products. Even where sufficient amount of crop by- products were more readily available, they represented but a small proportion in the diet of sheep and goats. For example, it was found in west

Java, Indonesia, that grasses represented 62-95 per cent of the small ruminants' diet under mixed farm conditions and crop by- products represented not more than 2-11 per cent even though such feeds were available in plenty (Van Eyes *et al.*, 1987)

Dependence on CPRs and uncultivated lands could be reduced if the small ruminants economy is maintained on stall feeding based on lopped/harvested fodder or commercial feeds. However, in doing so the private cost of small ruminants evonomy could be much more and many rural households particularly, the poor the landless may not be able to bear it. This is reflected in our finding about the economics of small ruminants. It may be recalled how the inclusion of the imputed cost of grazing made small ruminants keepers non-viable.

Futher, in a free range grazing system practised in the arid, semi-arid and droughtprone regions, where sheep and goats have become a part of the eco-system, common property resources and other uncultivated lands are very much important. Small, integrated crop-livestock farms have ample access to low-quality grasses and crop residuces that contain low (2-10%) concentrations of crude protein (CP) and high (65-75%) concentrations of (netural-detergent) cell well fibre (NDF). Such feeds are widely included in small ruminants diet (Van Eys *et. al.*, 1987)

Due to excessive degradation and shrinkage of CPRs and other uncultivated lands, the goats and sheep are subjected to two types of problems. First, they have to wander over a long distance in search of dry and unused grass, thorns and bushes for their survival. Second, they are being accused by the conservationists and environmentalists as the most destructive of vegetation. As far as the availability of grazing lands and fodder is concerned, it has been estimated that at the all India level the availability of permanent meadows and grass lands per animal unit (AU) was only 0.4 hectares. The availability of forages from permanent pastures, grass lands, road sides and communal lands was estimated at 1.5kg dry matter (DM) per animal unit per day (Van Eys, *et al.*, 1987, p. 54). Assuming only sheep and goats will graze/browse on these lands and taking the norm of fodder consumption by them as 3 per cent of their body weight, each animal need at least 0.75 kgs. of dry matter per day. Equating 5 small ruminants to one animal unit (AU), 3.75 kgs of dry matter is required per animal unit goats and sheep per day.[10] Thus a deficit of 2.25 kg dry matter, which shows that the availability is much less (less than 50 per cent) than the requirement of small ruminants. But actually the deficit could be even more since the large ruminants also graze on the CPRs and other grazing lands. The pressure on these lands by the large ruminants is much higher and their number is also higher. Large ruminants complete both for good quality-fodder and they require large areas for grazing. Goats and sheep are pushed to the margin and graze the left overs on marginal lands after the large ruminants are grazed. As a result of this the availability of dry matter for small ruminants could be much less than what is estimated above.

Based on the livestock census (1990) and the land utilization data (Government of Karnataka, 1989-90) it has been tried here to estimate the availability of grazing lands (pastures, forests, permanent fallows, barren, cultivable waste, uncultivable waste and other grazing lands) as well as the availability of dry matter (DM) per animal unit of small ruminants in Karnataka. Taking all the ruminants (cattle, buffaloes, goats and sheep) into account, the availability of grzing lands is only 0.34 hectares per animal unit. This shows the extent of pressure on grazing lands, against their carrying

---

10. One animals unit is equal to one bullock/one cow/one buffalo/ 5 goats/5 sheep. The average body weight of a sheep/goat is around 25 kgs. Cow, buffalo, goat and sheep consume the dry matter on free range grazing equal to around 3 per cent of their body weight.

capacity of 2.5 sheep per hectare or one cow per 2.4 to 4 hectares (Chakravarty, 1971, as quoted in Pandeya, 1988). If the large ruminants are exluded, the availability of these lands is much more for the small ruminants, being 3.15 hectares per animal unit. Gadgil and Sinha have estimated the dry matter yield from these lands as ranging from 1 to 2.5 tonnes per hectare per annum (Gadgil and Sinha, 1986). Taking the minimum yield of 1 tonne per hectare the availability of dry matter per animal unit of total ruminants is only 0.34 tonnes. As against this, the total requirement of dry matter by one animal unit of sheep and goats alone is around 1.36 tonnes per annum,—a deficit of more than one tonne! Further, the pressure, on grazing lands is much more by the large ruminants. Even if we assume only half of the available dry matter (0.17 tonnes) from these lands is consumed by the large ruminants (since they are also fed on crop residues), the other half could hardly meet the requirements of sheep and goats. Since small ruminants depend fully on these lands for their dry matter requirements face a severe crunch.

Availability of dry matter as well as grazing lands per animal unit has also been worked out at the micro/village level. In the study villages, as per the official accords for land use data and ruminant population as per our survey, the availability of grazing lands per animal unit of total ruminant livestock is around 0.70 hectare. But actually as per our survey around 50 per cent of the grazing lands (gomals and forests) have been brought under the plough both legally as well as illegally by way of encroachments. Thus a mere 0.35 hectare of grazing land per animal unit of total ruminant livestock is available now. Availability of dry matter per animal unit in our study villages is at the same level as at the state.

In a fragile environment where crop cultivation is a risky and uncertain proposition, livestock grazing is a productive land use system. Grazing and range land vegetation are co-adopted; both under grazing and over-grazing, resulting in the growth of woody plants and large, unpalatable grasses, reduce the productive potential of an area (World Bank 1991). Moderate grazing maintains soil fertility and physical soil characteristics. In fact grazing lands are regenerated when the seeds germinate which are passed through the digestive tract of the grazing animals. Excessive grazing (over use) results in the decline of required fodder species and increase unpalatable and woody species. It also loads to soil, water and wind erosion. Excess grazing by large ruminants like the cows scar hill sides and trigger an erosional process that may result in gully formation.

Traditionally, there have existed several grazing regimes like forests, grazing lands (gomals), tank beds and tank foreshores in the rural economies for many years. The man-livestock relationship depended also on the extent and type of different grazing regimes. Man-livestock relationship was for draught power, transport manure, milk meal and immediate cash through the sale of animals. Introduction of modern technology and the use of chemical power has led to some decline in this relationship in respect of draught power. However, inspite of the fact that chemical fertiliser and commercial dairying have also come into the picture, the traditional man-livestock relationship based on the need for manure and cash continues to exist. Commercialisation of crop cultivation has led to changed cropping pattern with low fodder base. The degradation and shrinkage of CPRs made it difficult to maintain the large ruminants like cows and buffaloes. Since the CPRs continue to decline, competition between man, large ruminants and small ruminants for the available resources increase further. This may lead to the ultimate collapse of the whole grazing regime.

One may not find any grazing cycle now in the villages as it was normally practised in the recent past (Damodaran, 1987). There was a system of grazing ruminant livestock in different seasons. For example, immediately after the crops are harvested grazing was allowed on stubbles. Tank foreshores and tank beds were used for grazing during summer when there could be no water in the tanks. Common grazing lands (gomals) and forests etc. were largely used during the kharif season. It has been reported by the villagers that in the past apart from following the grazing cycle, the system of herd movement was also ecologically sound. All the herders use to move towards the grazing leads in a group usually at a particular time and come back in the same manner. While grazing the herder used to keep the cows in front which are followed by goats and Sheep. Due to the changed social structure of the village society, shrinkage and degradation of grazing lands, changed cropping pattern etc., the system of grazing cycle as well as sound management of the flock/herd has broken down.

As far as the grazing habits are concerned sheep are grazers whereas goats are browsers. When there is scarcity of fodder from bushes, plants and trees, goats adapt themselves for grazing of the small grasses. Sheep graze very close to the ground and out the grass to the bottom. Unlike other ruminant livestock, goats move very fast from plant to plant and from one bush to the other. If there is good vegetation consisting of thorny bushes, leguminous plants, fodder trees etc., goats never stay on a particular place unlike the other ruminants. Goat like the tender leaves and do not uproot the plant nor trample it. Only when it finds shortage of fodder from bushes, plants and trees it becomes a grazer and eats away whatever is available. If it is small grass or a plant, it kneels down on its front legs and with the help of its mobile lips, tongue and sharp teeth pull the grass/plant with its roots. Here it really becomes an enemy of vegetation as alleged by foresters and conservationists. In fact all types of ruminant livestock are dangerous to the vegetation if they are not properly managed along with the sound management of the grazing leads. Among the ruminant livestock goats are blamed much for the, destruction of the vegetation particularly, in a fragile environment. This may be because of the grazing habit of the goats. Unlike cows, buffaloes and sheep, goals never starve much for fodder or water. When severe shortage of fodder and water is felt particularly during the time of droughts, goats live much longer than cows, buffaloes and sheep. Goats are hardy and active animals. Goats have often been seen standing on their hind limbs near a compound wall and eating a flower plant with the help of their mobile neck, tongue and the upper lip. They try to get the fodder and water from all the possible sources.

In the study region goats are normally grazed in forests, on hill slopes, on grazing lands and road sides.Generally goats are grazed by boys and girls who are physically fit. In many cases if the herd is large, able bodied male members manage the grazing of goats. Sheep are grazed normally on tank beds, tank foreshore, gomals (grazing lands), hill sides, farm bunds and road sides. Often they are also taken to nearby forests. Since sheep are grazing animals prefer some or the other type of grass as their diet. Normally they are grazed by the aged, women and children. Sheep are much less harmful to the vegetation as well as to the crops as compared with large ruminants. But when there is serve shortage of grass or if they are forced to graze on small grass, they graze very close to the soil leading to severe soil erosion.

The grazing system practiced in the study region could be categorised as semi -intensive. Households maintain goats and sheep as a subsidiary source of income and as a complementary activity to farming. Goats and sheep are taken out of the house by a member of the family in the morning and bring them back in the evening. Herders travel with their animals upto 8-10 kilometers a day during summer. During rainy season they travel much less as they get the required dry matter for their animals around the walking distance. There is no system of seasonal migration of goats arid sheep to the other regions as practised in other and and semi-arid areas of the country. Goats and sheep are let lose in the forests or on the CPRs and the herder keeps a constant vigil on their movements. As a help the goats and sheep herders maintain one or two local dogs well trained to carefully watch the grazing and movements of goals and sheep. They also watch the goats and sheep against the predators. Normally during the mid day all the herders assemble along with their herd/flocks at a particular place around a water point. Goats and sheep too defer browsing/grazing for sometime. The practice also help the mating of goats and sheep, as many herders do not maintain any buck on ram. Even the herders need some rest under a tree as they travel since morning along with goats and sheep. Particularly it is more helpful during rainy season and severe summer. Many herders have reported of sun strokes and continued health problems as they have to travel a very long distance particularly along with the goats. Due to continued felling of big trees they hardly get a proper shelter to take some rest atleast during the mid day. Only adult animals (above 3 and 4 months) are taken out for grazing/browsing. The lambs/kids below 3 or 4 months old are left at home and some lopped fodder is fed. The kids/lambs join their mothers only when the flock/herd come back after the days grazing/ browsing. Ther herder keeps the flock/herd inside a house.

8.3 Social Cost and Private Cost of their Economy and the Dependence on Common Property Resources

Economic efficiency of a proposition could be judged based on net returns. Net returns could be positive as well as negative as per the extent and type of input costs involved in the production process. All economic activities will have positive as well as negative externalities. Social costs arise on account of negative externalities. Externalities are so termed because they are external to the market trading process, but they are not external to the ecological process (Batie, 1989). Depletion of renewable and non renewable resources, pollution and ecological degradation as a result of the production process constitute negative externalities. Externalities arise on account of institutional failures. Current property rights neither provide incentives to protect the environment nor to protect the rights of minority cultures (Batie, 1989). The producer's interest is to maximise the returns without any concern for externalities. When an economic activity depends largely on free inputs from natural resources, the social cost in terms of negative externalities borne by the society at large could be significant. But, in such cases the producers account only the private, costs like cost of his own labour used and 'out of the pocket' expenses incurred in the production of a commodity.

The sheep and goats keepers too try to maximise their returns with minimum 'out of the pocket' expenses. Small ruminants economy depend to a considerable extent on CPRs which include forests, grazing lands (gomals), tank beds, tank foreshores, road sides, bunds etc. As we have mentioned earlier the only key inputs used in goats and sheep rearing was human labour and fodder from CPRS. Own labour is used rather excessively since the opportunity cost of such labour is zero/negligible and it is also used in other household activities.

The private cost of small ruminants economy include the paid out cost incurred on animal health, transportation charges of animals to the market place, hired labour charges paid and the imputed cost of family labour. The imputed value of dry matter consumed by the small ruminants on CPRs is accounted as social cost. Though there is no market for the dry matter consumed by goats and sheep on CPRS, we have valued it at 50 per cent of the selling price of crop residues from low quality coarse cereals in the study villages. The quality of dry matter from CPRs is much low as compared with even the low quality crop residues. We assume that if there was a market for dry matter consumed by goats and sheep the herders would have had to pay for it. We consider it as social cost since the individual herder's stock graze on the common property without paying anything for its use. It is also a cost to the society since the use and abuse of CPRs by the individual herder may affect the private property resource (land) of the society in terms of soil erosion and siltation.

Dry matter collected or grazed by sheep and goats from CPRs outside the market framework benefit only the individual herder. It has been widely reported by the rural households that since the sheep and goats herders need not have to pay for the key input-fodder, they prefer to maintain the small ruminants even at marginal return. In the past, the economy of small ruminants flourished in the rural areas only because of the abundant availability of CPRs. Apart from the low pressure on CPRs from other ruminant livestock, the availability of these resources in relation to the demand was much more. As a result of which the burden of social cost of small ruminants grazing on CPRs was not felt much. In fact one can argue that in an eco-system with sound ecological balance, grazing of goats and sheep on CPRs may not have any social cost at all. In turn the benefits to the society are much more as rearing goats and sheep by the poor and landless. based on CPRs with promote equity at large. Particularly more so in arid and semi-arid region where the income earning opportunities are loss and crop cultivation becomes a risky and uncertain proposition. Further, in a system where small ruminants are maintained largely on unused grasses, bushes, thorns etc. there may not be any cost to the society. But social cost of small ruminants grazing could be much more if these animals are grazed excessively in large numbers on degraded CPRs. Particularly where afforestation and regeneration of such lands has been taken up, uncontrolled grazing by goats and sheep may lead to further degradation. Sustainability of the developed area could be achieved through rotational grazing of different plots by different species of ruminant livestock along with maintaining their carrying capacity.

In order to reduce the social cost of small ruminants grazing on CPRs, goats and sheep can be maintained on stall feeding. The herders can lop/harvest the fodder/grass from the developed CPRs and feed their animals. They can also maintain goats and sheep on commercial feeds and fodder as being done in the case of crossbreed cows and buffaloes. In both the cases the herder's private cost may go up which many households particularly the poor and landless could not afford. To lop/harvest the fodder/grass, the herders may also have to spend more time. Many herders lack enough place to keep their animals and to stall feed them. Nevertheless, goats can he maintained to some extent on stall feeding if they are both milk and meat animals. For this, however, genetic upgradation of local goats is essential. High milk yielding goats with high prolificacy could be easily adopted for stab feeding by the rural households. This could also control deforestation and reduce the social costs. But even this may not be possible unless the CRPs are protected, regenerated and used in a sustainable way, because it is the fodder from CPRs which would have to be the major source for even stall feeding through collection of grass instead of direct grazing. In the absence of good quality CPRs, the input cost particularly of feed and fodder could be much high and the rural households may not maintain oven the high-yielding prolific breeds of goats. Maintaining sheep on stall feeding for commercial purpose could be much more difficult as the economics of these animals is favourable to the herders only when they are maintained on CPRs. Even in areas with high irrigation and lesser/no CPRs, sheep are maintained on stubbles and road side herbages.

8.4 Factors Affecting Efficiency, Sustainability and Equity

In small ruminants activity efficiency, sustainability and equity are closely inter-related. Efficiency depends to a large extent on the sustainable use of CPRs, which are the base of the key input (fodder) used in this activity. Return from goats and sheep could he increased if CPRs are managed and used in a sustainable way. The degradation and abuse of CPRs has led to the decline in net returns from goats and sheep. As these animals graze intensively on the degraded CPRs, they have to spend most of their energy in travelling over the CPRs to get their required dry matter. This has led to further degradation of CPRs along with the decline in returns from small ruminants. Efficiency also depend on the sound management and care of goats and sheep. Poor veterinary facilities affect the growth of these animals, particularly when they are subject to diseases. Many times herders suffer a sudden and huge, loss due to unnoticed diseases or late diagnosis of the illness of goats and sheep. Lack of proper management and health care like regular dipping, de-worming washing etc. also affects the economic efficiency of small ruminants activity. Sustainability of both small ruminants activity and the CPRs will help in achieving the sustainable development of the region. Positive net returns from small ruminants along with good quality CPRs with help increased return from farming and hence total income and employment will also increase. For the sustainable use and management of CPRs appropriate and efficient local institutional arrangements are required. Due to commercialisation of the village economy, technological changes and the changed social pattern of the rural families, the traditional system of collective management and use of CPRs has broken down. The attitude now is more towards establishing private (self) ownership of CPRs rather than maintaining them as CPRs. This has adversely affected agriculture as well as animal husbandry making both these economies less sustainable.

The poor and the landless have a very low access to land and capital and hence concentrate on allied activities like small ruminants rearing based on CPRs, which require low or negligible cash expenses. As long as CPRs and free labour are available, the poor and the landless can have some relative advantage in keeping small ruminants over the rich households. Rich households concentrate much more on crop cultivation and other allied activities like dairying, business etc. The system of stubble grazing by the goats and sheep of poor and landless on the rich farmers' field was much helpful to the poor and landless. Though this may enrich the crop fields of the rich, it also provided as assured and good source of fodder to the goats and sheep of the poor and landless. Apart from the introduction of new technologies into agriculture and the double cropping, a change in the social environment has affected this practice. Stubbles grazed by the small ruminants of the poor and landless are now grazed by the own animals of rich peasants. There is much more individualism today than earlier, and the community ethos and interdependence between different rual communities which prevailed in the past has almost completely broken down and is replaced by market relationships. All this has affected the poor and the landless to a considerable extent. It has become more difficult than in the past for the poor and landless to maintain few goats and sheep on the available CPRs. That is how the rich peasants now tend to keep more small ruminants than the poor, and the economies of scale also favour the rich. The only way of turning them in favour of the poor lies through rehabilitating CPRs. Poverty allviation programmes should therefore incorporate concrete plans to protect and develop the available CPRs through active involvement and participation of all the rural households particularly the poor. It is not enough to provide small ruminants or cows to the poor under IRDP and such programmes, without ensuring free or cheap fodder for these animals. New institutional arrangements could be evolved to improve the access of the poor to CPRs along with improving their productivity. Sound management and care of small ruminants need special attention. All that requires a re-thinking about the neglected sector of small ruminants economy.

9 CONCLUSION AND IMPLICATIONS

9.1 Highlights of the Study

Droughtprone or arid and semi-arid areas pose special problems due to their limited resource endowments like low and uncertain rainfall, low yield in crop production, low fodder base and hence ill-health and low productivity from livestock. Concentrating on crop cultivation alone may not be enough to develop these areas. The role of animal husbandry becomes relevant, particularly in diversifying the rural economy of these areas and providing additional source of income.

Under animal husbandry, a lion's share of allocation of development programmers has gone to schemes like 'operation flood' oriented to cows and buffaloes, *i.e.*, to large ruminants. These programmes, however, may not suit all arid and semi-arid areas due to limited fodder resources available there. The role of small ruminants (goats and sheep) in general and in arid and semi-arid areas in particular needs greater attention. In droughtprone areas, rearing of small ruminants helps the rural households to survive better during and after droughts. Small ruminants require much less foddder than large ruminants. They can flourish without any concentrated food. Income from the rearing of small ruminants can also be substantially high. Goats and sheep may cause some destruction to the environment but only when they are raised without any controlled management.

The focus of this study is on the economies of small ruminants in a droughtprone or semi-arid region. This has been carried out mainly from the point of individual households as decision making units in terms of their self interest. But this has also been supplemented by an analysis of the natural and marketing environment faced by these households and the interaction between the households economy and the village environment. While our methodology of studying the economics of small ruminants has followed the neo-classical approach to production economics at the micro level, our approach has also taken into account how this economics of small ruminants is differentiated by the rural class structure. Economics of small ruminants is studied in broader terms including inter-class differences, social costs and environmental considerations. It has been studied mainly through three angles or dimensions-efficiency including capacity for survival in the face of risk, sustainability and equity. These dimensions are also very closely inter-related.

In this connection, the costs and returns in the rearing of small ruminants across different class of households and across different flock/herd sizes have been studied. We have adopted the cost concepts in our study which are used in agriculture by the Farm Management Studies and subsequently revised and recommended by the committee chaired by Professor S.R. Sen. We have used them with some modification as some more costs, those arising out of risk bearing and social costs, had also to be considered. The cost concepts used by us are:

Cost A1 = All paid out cost (cash and kind), value of own fodder used, transportation and other miscellaneous expenses;

Cost A2 = A1 + rent paid on share cropping;

Cost B1 = A2 + Interest on owned capital assets (livestock) excluding land;

Cost Br = B1 + risk premium;

Cost C1 = B1 + imputed value of family labour;

Cost Cr = C1 + risk premium;

Cost Cs = Cr + imputed value of free grazing (Social costs).

Further, we have derived the gross returns from animal husbandry as follows:

GR = NC + TS – P + CS + RD + OR

Where : NC = Net change in the value of the livestock;

TS = Total proceeds from sale of animals;

P = Expenditure on purchase of animals;

CS = Consumption of animals at source;

RD = Returns from dead animals;

OR = Other returns (value of manure, wool, milk, skin, etc).

We have tried to understand the relationship between common property resources (CPRs) and small ruminant production, particularly from the point of view of the growing concern of degradation of these land by the grazing of small ruminants. The social costs of small ruminants rearing could be different from the private costs, where there is dependence on common property resources. This is particularly so because there are no institutional arrangements at present in the studied village to make a sustainable use of CPRs such a through rotational grazing and rotational enclosure of parts of CPRs to grow desired fodder. Apart from production and environmental aspects, the marketing aspects of small ruminants and their products at the household and at the village level are also studied.

In the state of Karnataka we have selected Kolar district as our study region. Kolar district is a droughtprone region with low level of irrigation. It ranks first in the state in terms of small ruminants per 100 rural households and second in terms of density of small ruminants per sq.km. Further, Bagepalli Taluka in Kolar district has been selected for the detailed study. In Bagepalli taluka we have selected three contiguous village—Achepalli, Neergantpalli, and gurraldinne, purposively, where we find large concentration of small ruminants with a relatively low level of agricultural activities. A total of 102 households with small ruminants from the three villages have been studied. We covered all households which had small ruminants in these villages. Detailed household data were collected for one year period from April 1987 to March 1988. Field work was carried out during four months from March to June, 1988.

The households data have been analysed in two ways, across class of farmers and across flock/herd size. The study is based both on secondary as well as primary data. Secondary data have been collected from the official records and published reports and documents.

We have categorized households with small ruminants into three classes as follows:

1. Rich Peasants,
2. Poor Peasants, and
3. Landless Labour.

The rich peasants do not hire-out any labour, but only hire-in. They use own labour in self-employment, which the other two classes also do including landless labout, the latter doing it for animals husbandry but not for cultivation. The two poor classes also hire-in some labour, particularly for tending livestock, but labour hired-out by them far exceeds labour hire-in. Though both hire-out, labour the difference between the two is that the former have some land, while the latter do not have any except homesteads.

Sheep and goats play a relatively important role in Karnataka as compared with the country. Karnataka ranked 4th in sheep meat production in India, contributing around 10 per cent of total sheep meat production in the country. In goat meat production it stood 10th by contributing around 5 per cent to total goat meat production. In total meat production, the share of sheep and goats is important. In Karnataka during 1978-79 the share of sheep and goat meat to total meat production was 66 per cent and which has gone up to 70 per cent during 1995-96. Further, between 1978-79 and 1995-96 total mutton and goat meat production has increased by more than 600 per cent points.

Numerically, cattle dominate livestock; small ruminants formed 37.7 per cent of total ruminants livestock in Karnataka during 1990, which was almost the same as about 37 per cent in the country as a whole during 1992. In Karnataka sheep population has increased by 15 per cent between 1956 to 1990 as against 30 per cent in the country as a whole. Goats population has increased more than cattle and sheep both in Karnataka and in India. It has increased by 50 per cent in Karnataka and by 108 per cent in India during the same period.

The significance of small ruminants for droughtprone areas is evident from the fact while they constituted 44 per cent of total ruminants in these districts, their share was only 12.5 per cent in non-droughtprone districts in Karnataka during 1990. On the other hand, cattle dominate in the non-droughtprone districts accounting for 65 per cent of total ruminants during the same year, compared to only 41 per cent in droughtprone districts. In terms of comparable animal units per hectare of grazing lands, the pressure, on grazing lands (CPRs) by the large ruminants (*i.e.,* 12.5 units per hectare) is much more than the pressure by small ruminants (which was only 2 units per hectare) in droughtprone districts. This is inspite of relatively greater significance of small ruminants in droughtprone areas. The figures only show how exaggerated are the fears regarding the destructive capacity of small ruminants from the point of deforestation.

It may be recalled that our sample is biased in favour of small ruminants, since we selected areas as well as households with small ruminants. Therefore, the estimates of contribution of animal husbandry from these households cannot be taken to be representative for all rural areas. Nevertheless our sample showed that agriculture still contributed a major part (63.4 per cent) to the total net returns (net of cost A2 only) of the rich peasants, and animal husbandry's share was 32.9 per cent. Sheep and goats were not a major source of income to these households, since only about 18 per cent of the total net returns came from these animals. In the economy of poor peasants, animals husbandry's share to total households net returns was more significant, being 34.9 per cent. 21 per cent of their net returns came from small ruminants. Around 28 per cent of their total net returns constitute the share on account of hiring-out their labour. On the other hand, around 54 per cent of the total net returns of the landless households came from animal husbandry. The small ruminants' contribution to their total net returns was 29.1 per cent. Hiring out of own labour accounts for more than 41 per cent of their total net returns. This would show that even in areas with small ruminants, their role in general is secondary, but their relative significance to poor peasants and landless labour is more than that for rich peasants.

Labour and fodder (including free fodder from CPRs) are the only important inputs in the economy of small ruminants. They also explained more than 65 per cent of the variation in total returns from small ruminants in the regression analysis. Own labour constituted the major part of total labour used. Being free, own labour was found to be used beyond economical limit. At the margin, an additional rupee worth of labour (total) used, added less than a rupee worth of output. Since the opportunity cost of own labour is zero/negligible, even this low marginal value product is attractive for small ruminant rearers. Though this is amenable to be interpreted as a situation of disguised unemployment in the study region, it is more a case of raising the productivity rather than withdrawing the number of persons engged in small ruminant rearing. Such an increase in productivity can be achieved mainly through improving the nutrition and health of animals.

In small ruminants activity, Common Property Resources (CPRs) like grazing lands (gomals), tank beds, foreshores, forests, road sides etc., play a very important role. Even in their present degraded state, the marginal value product (MVP) of fodder grazed by goats and sheep on CPRs was substantial, being Rs. 469 per tonne and statistically significant at one per cent level. There is considerable scope to increase the productivity of CPRs through proper management and care, which will also help increased returns from small ruminants.

Net returns from small ruminants over the most comprehensive cost concept, Cs, are negative across all types of households except in the case of rich peasants where they are positive, being Rs. 340 and Rs. 11 per household and per animal respectively. If this cost had to be actually paid, the small ruminant economy would not have survived. But covering all the costs, including the imputed value of grazing on CPRs, is important in the long run so that the small ruminant economy is sustainable. This is particularly because at the present rate of use of CPRs, they may not continue to give the same amount of free inputs of fodder, unless there is some investment of effort and money in their regeneration. Net return over Cost Br, however, are positive and substantial both per household as well as per animal across all classes of rural households. This means that all paid-out costs and risk premium are covered by the gross returns. If imputed value of family labour is added to costs, *i.e.*, over costs C1 and Cr, the net returns per animal are positive in the case of rich peasants (Rs. 37 and Rs. 30 respectively) as well as landless labour (Rs. 13 and Rs. 7 respectively). They are negative, (being Rs. (–) 21 and Rs. (–) 27 per animal over cost C1 and Cr, respectively) in the case of poor peasants. Evidently, own labour is being used more freely among poor peasants than among the other two classes

Across flock/herd sizes the net returns per animal are positive over cast Cs (being Rs. 15 per animal) when the flock/herd size constitute more than 31 animals. With the flock/herd size up to 10 and between 11 to 30, net returns per animal over cost Cs become negative, begin Rs. (–) 71 and Rs. (–) 38, respectively. This shows that as the flock/herd size increases net returns per animal over cost C1, Cr and Cs also increases. Over cost Br it is the lowest size group (flock/herd size upto 10 animals) where the net returns per animal are substantial (Rs. 141) as compared with the size group of 11 to 30 and 31 and above, (being Rs. 83 and Rs. 85, respectively). These results show that small herds are economical in terms of paid out costs along and that the economics of small ruminants is more favourable to rich rather than poor peasants and the landless. Nevertheless, the latter maintain some small ruminants, even if well below economic optimum, as the returns over paid-out costs are positive for them in terms of which it is economical to hold even small herds. Though the level of economic viability varies accroding to the cost concept employed, viability in the long run on a sustainable basis can be only in terms of the most comprehensive cost concepts which includes risk premium and social costs, *i.e.,* cost Cs. This means that the long run viability of the small ruminant economy of the poor and landless could be ensured only at public cost or subsidies to maintain the free flow of fodder from grazing lands, or through efforts outside the market framework involving co-operation and efforts from beneficiaries.

Among small ruminants, goats were numerically more dominant accounting for over 64 per cent, with sheep accounting for less than 36 per cent. The proportion of goats was even higher, being 75 per cent among the poor peasants and 100 per cent among the landless, compared to 56 per cent among the rich. The share of gross returns from goats total returns from small ruminants was higher (being 70.1 per cent) than from sheep, being only 29.9 per cent. Further gross returns per animal were higher from goats (Rs. 131) as compared with sheep (Rs. 101). Though the net returns from sheep *vis-a-vis* goats over cost Cs were negative, they were much less from goats than sheep. Over all other costs net return were positive and much more from goats than sheep.

Based on total costs and total returns an attempt was made to identify the range of operation for the operator to obtain positive net returns from small ruminants. For this purpose, an attempt was made to relate total returns and total cost on the one hand, with flock/herd size on the other by using a cubic relationship, except in the case of total costs (TCBr), where we have used the linear relationship. The intercept for total costs (TCBr) function was lower than the intercept for total returns. Hence identification of the range of positive net returns by equating TR and TCBr did not arise. Setting TR – TCr = 0 (similarly TR – TCs = 0), and solving for X (flock size) the range of operation with positive returns can be obtained. Following this procedure, it was found that the operator has to perform within the range of 28 to 147 animals to get positive returns in terms of cost Cr, and 38 to 139 animals in terms of cost Cs. Below the size of 28 animals in terms of Cr and 38 animals in terms of Cs, the total returns are less than total cost and it is uneconomical. Similarly, beyond 147 animals in terms of Cr and 139 animals in terms of Cs, the total cost would exceed total returns.

To identify the flock/herd size at which the net returns are optimum the marginal returns and marginal cost were worked out. Taking into account all costs including the social cost the optimum level of returns are achieved when the flock/herd size constitute 101 animals, where marginal costs are equal to marginal returns and the former begin to exceed the latter. On cost Cr *i.e.* total cost excluding the social cost, the optimum level of returns are achieved when the flock/herd size constitute 104 animals where the marginal cost is equal to marginal return beyond which marginal cost exceeds marginal revenue. It may be noted that the difference between the two optimum points in respect of the two cost concepts, *viz.,* between 101 and 104, is not high. Whether imputed costs of grazing are included or not, the maximum profits are made at the flock/herd size of around 100.

On cost Br, *i.e.,* all paid out costs (Cash & Kind), imputed value of own fodder used, interest on capital (small ruminants) and the risk premium, but excluding the imputed cost of own labour used and the imputed cost of free grazing on CPRs, the optimum level of returns are achieved when the flock/herd size constitute 119 animals where MC and MR curves intersect each other. Beyond this point marginal cost begins to be more than the marginal returns. It should also be noticed that on cost Br, the operator gets positive net returns even at one animal. That is to say, including all costs except the imputed cost of own labour and fodder from CPRs, maintaining even one animal becomes viable economically. But from our analysis we cannot say anything about the maximum size of flock/herd, beyond which the total returns are less than the total cost TCBr. In other words we cannot say anything about the range of positive net returns over TCBr.

Our analysis shows that to get *optimum* returns from goats and sheep, the small ruminant keepers should have a little above 100 animals. This is so in terms of cost Cs, Cr as well as Br. From the point of view of micro level economics, *i.e.,* from the point of a household, such a recommendation may be acceptable. But if all the goat the sheep keepers increase their stock to the optimum size, it may have an adverse effect on CPRs leading to the tragedy of the commons, unless and supply of fodder from CPRs is made elastic enough to meet the increasing need of fodder through special efforts. Nevertheless, the goat and sheep keepers maintain the flock/herd size at sub-optimum level, since on paid out costs it is economical to have even one animal. Since only two households maintained small ruminants above the herd size of hundred, we had to analyse the characteristics of relatively more efficient and less efficient households in terms of the level of output-input ratios for comparison. There were hardly enough observations in the category of households who could be said to have attained the optimum size in respect of small ruminants. After arranging the total households in descending order of output/input[11] ratios, 25 per cent of the households from above were identified as the most efficient households and the 25 per cent at the bottom as the least efficient. Some of their characteristics were also identified. White 21.6 per cent of rich peasants were in the most efficient category, only 5.4 per cent of them were the least efficient. In contrast, 26.2 per cent of the poor peasants were in the most efficient but 37.7 per cent of them were in the least efficient. This suggests the relative dominance of the poor peasants among the least efficient. The average size of land holding of the most efficient group was 4.27 acres while that of the least efficient was 2.11 acres. The former also had larger area under irrigation. The average herd/flock size of small ruminant holding of the most efficient was also larger, being 16 compared to 10 in the case of the least efficient. The most efficient group *owned* small ruminants as compared with the least efficient households who were also share croppers. The most efficient group operated their animals much more through hired labour as compared with the least efficient group, while the least efficient group used more of own labour as compared with most efficient households.

Small ruminants depend fully on CPRs for grazing, though stubble grazing also contribute to their fodder requirements. Due to commercialisation of agriculture, population pressure, changes in the village level informal institutions and the changed perceptions and attitudes of the rural households towards CPRs, the CPRs either have gone into the hands of individual households as private property resources or exist in a very bad condition (heavy degradation) due to their

11. Inputs are taken in terms of Cost Cr.

abuses. As a result of this, returns from small ruminants seem to be declining atleast in real terms. Though small ruminants travel a very long distance in the forests or on road sides for grazing, they hardly meet their required quality and quantity of fodder the whole year. Due to lack of proper nutrition the small ruminants are also subject to many diseases. Added to this due to the very poor veterinary facilities in the study region, the small ruminant keepers are exposed to risks of heavy losses.

Local breeds of sheep and goats are less productive and less prolific animals. Average body weight of an adult live animal is less than 30 kgs as compared with 90 to 100 kgs in the case of the high quality breeds in other parts of the country as well as in the world. Goats are not milked in the study region. Average realisable yield of milk per doe per day during the lactation period of 3 to 4 months is hardly about 50 grams (net of milk suckled by the kid/s) for the existing varieties, which is also allowed to be suckled by the kid/s. This is miserably low in comparison with high milk yielding goats like Jamnapari, Beetal, Anglo- Nubion etc., which yield on an average about 2 to 4 liters of milk a day. Yield of wool from the sheep is also very low. Local sheep are not wool yielding animals. On an average each sheep yield hardly 500 to 750 grams of coarse wool per annum. Some times is not at all sheared by the farmers for about 2 to 3 years. Coarse wool is used in the manufacturing of local blankets called 'Kamblis'.

Goats and sheep keepers face the problem of marketing of both small ruminants as well as their by- products. There is no well organised marketing system for small ruminants in the study region. Farmers have to travel a long distance to market their animals in the weekly/monthly shandies. While travelling with the animals, as well as till the animals are sold in the shandies, they face the problem of fodder and water to their animals. As a result of which the body weight of the animals decreases and they lose substantial returns. Many households sell their animals within the village to the middlemen rather than face risks and problems of the market places (shandies). The middlemen, both from within the village as well as from other areas, exploit the sheep and goat keepers by fixing the rate per animals or per flock/herd based on rough estimates of their weight.

9.2 Implications for the Family

In the economy of rural households particularly of the poor and landless, raising goats and sheep can act as an hedge against risk and uncertainty. In droughtprone or semi-arid regions since both crop cultivation as well as maintaining large ruminants are subjected to frequent losses, maintaining goats and sheep compensate for such losses to a considerable extent. Due to the continued excess use and abuse of grazing lands and other CPRs small ruminants activity too is becoming more and more inefficient. Though economics of scale and optimum size favour maintaining larger size of herds than at present, this is severely constrained by the availability of CPRs and fodder from them. Let alone maintaining large herds, even keeping a couple of goats or sheep has become difficult particularly for the poor and landless. Only the rich can afford to keep larger herds since they can use their own lands for stubble grazing. The traditional complementarity between large farmers and ruminants keepers, whereby the small ruminants of the latter used to graze on the fields of the former after harvesting, has weakened. Both due to this and thanks to the shrinkage and degradation of grazing lands and other CPRs and economies of scale favouring larger herds, goats and sheep could no longer be associated with the poor. This is the paradox. Even an activity which has a good potential for supporting the livelihood of the poor, gets concentrated in the hands of the non-poor. Only a regeneration and sustainable management of CPRs could help the poor in improving their resource base to support small ruminants.

Small ruminants are an integral part of many farming

families, and hence a reduction in returns from them will affect the whole economic system of such households. Rural households maintain goats and sheep as part of their overall survival strategy. Returns from goats and sheep could be increased if these animals are managed property. The poor quality breeds could be improved by crossing them with high yielding good quality breeds from other parts of the country as well as from the world. Genetic upgradation of goats and sheep along with sustainable use of CPRs and other grazing lands, could enhance the returns from small ruminants.

9.3 Implications for the Community

Though small ruminants are owned by the individual households they are maintained on public or community resources like grazing lands and other CPRs. Herders pay nothing for the use of such resources. Formal or informal institutional arrangement within the local communities can enable a sustainable use of these resources. These institutional arrangements may have to ensure rotational grazing to allow for regeneration, and also allow the growth of fodder trees to allow some amount of supplementary stall feeding so that the grazing pressure could be reduced. An efficient management of goat and sheep along with a sustainable and equitable use of CPRs will promote equity in rural areas, as many poor and landless families can also maintain these animals. This would require participatory forms of institutions for the management of CPRs where each household has equal rights, not necessarily proportional to herd size. Village communities can evolve norms and conventions for equitable distribution of produce of CPRs along with rotational grazing.

Small ruminants along with other types of ruminant livestock should be maintained as per the carrying capacity of the local rangelands/CPRs. To control the number of ruminants, expecially the unproductive large ruminants which are nevertheless as source of pressure on the commons, local communities can levy a tax per head of animal on large ruminants. This can help local communities to finance the regeneration of CPRs, and will have the desirable effect of reducing the number of cattle whose productivity to the owners is less than the amount of the tax. Such a tax—but at a lower rate—can be extended to small ruminants in the case of non-poor peasant households owning more than one hectare of land. It may be recalled that such peasants recover even the cost Cs which is inclusive of the imputed value of free grazing. As such, this tax will not be an undue burden on them, and will at the same time help financing the regeneration of CPRs and regulate the number of animals. Such a tax should be levied by local institutions and spent for local benefits only. Further, in meeting the continued urban demand for small ruminants and their products the goat and sheep keepers can act together co-operatively to improve their bargaining with urban middlemen. This need not necessarily be through a formal establishment of co-operatives, but even through informal association. Similarly, the local communities can arrange for veterinary care by cost sharing on collective basis. Each herder could be trained to give first-aid and motivated to keep a first-aid box, so that he can treat the disease affected animals immediately. Indigenous knowledge of herbal medicines to treat animals should also be promoted and shared. Local communities should ensure that herbs used to treat animals do not become extinct.

9.4 Implications for Public Policy

Government has several anti-poverty programmes to develop the semi-arid regions in general and the poor and landless in particular. The poor and landless are also financed at subsidized rate for small units of sheep and goats. But this requires maintenance of CPRs and their sustainable use. On the other hand, the government is lax in protecting the CPRs and allows regularisation of encroachments on them merrily. The encroachments are often by the rich peasants themselves, for they alone have the political strength to do it and ensure regularisation. There is thus a contradiction in the policy of government which gives easy loans to the poor to acquire small ruminants on the one hand, and allows privatisation of CPRs on the other. The strategy of the government to improve the economic condition of the poor and landless by strengthening their asset base through animal husbandry could be in vain unless the CPRs are protected and regenerated in which the government has an important role.

But merely preventing privatisation of CPRs is not enough. To check the damage on environment and ecology caused by goats and sheep, particularly in afforested areas, some amount of stall feeding can be encouraged. To make stall feeding affordable, the government, particularly the Forest Department should give greater attention to growing fodder trees and grass on their lands, so that local communities find it possible to cut fodder and feed the animals instead of directly grazing them. Since complete stall feeding is neither desirable nor feasible, forests and such other uncultivated lands could be used for grazing on a rotational basis. Goats and sheep maintained on free grazing are adaptable to the eco-system of the arid and semi-arid regions. They are hardy as well as drought and disease resistant. Stall fed animals need assured supply of fodder of good quality and water. They are also more susceptible to diseases. In semi-arid regions maintaining large herds of small ruminants on stall feeding could be difficult since many families lack good housing as well as assured supply of water and fodder. Experience shows that even the stall feeding of cross bred cows was not successful in many areas. There is therefore no sense in completely banning grazing in CPRs and forest lands. The government could encourage local communities to evolve practices of combining stall feeding with planned and rotational grazing on its lands, involving local people in their management. Wherever some amount of stall feeding of goats and sheep could be possible, it should be supplemented with free/cheap fodder in the rural areas.

CPRs can be managed for sustainable and productive use and their cost of management could be charged to the users. If there is no management of CPRs at all, and high returns from small ruminants are used only for private benefit without regenerating CPRs, even the high returns that meet imputed cost of free fodder, by themeslves do not automatically ensure sustainable use of CPRs. In the case of poor peasants and landless labour since the returns from small ruminants are not high enough to cover the imputed cost of free fodder, cost of regeneration and sustainable management of CPRs may have to be subsided and cannot be charged fully to them. On the other hand the net returns over all comprehensive costs (including the imputed cost of free fodder) from small ruminants are positive in the case of rich peasants, a certain amount of cost of regeneration and sustainble management of CPRs could be charged to them. But this requires full participation of all the rural households. It may be clarified that such a cost recovery from rich peasants can be met in the form of a tax or charge as proposed in the preceding section. Such a cost recovery is not proposed in addition to a charge per animal.

Some thought has to be given for achieving genetic up-gradation of goats and sheep, without disturbing their genetic diversity and resistance to droughts and disease. Research and development activities on goats and sheep should be taken as a part of the state policy. To meet the continued demand for milk and meat from the growing human population, genetic upgradation of goats and sheep is essential. Since there is a taboo as far as the beef and buffaloe meat consumption is concerned, there exist a considerable scope to increase the meat production from small ruminants in India. Raising the milk potential of goats has the potential of strengthening the economy of rural housholds, particularly of poor and landless as well as raising their dietary levels. In order to promote efficiency in small ruminants activity, a good system of veterinary facilities should be created in rural areas. Apart from promoting such facilities in terms of western practice, the local knowledge of herbal medicine should be properly documented, researched and promoted. Proper preventive care is also essential.

Middlemen still control the trade of goats and sheep as well as their by-products and hence exploit both the primary producers as well as the consumers. Promoting an efficient marketing system along with good infrastructure facilities could limit their role. This would require dissemination of information on prices and facilities available. Ensuring a greater share in the consumer price to the small ruminant keepers could also promote efficiency in the rearing of small ruminants along with protecting the interest of consumers.

Small ruminants still have a good potential of being used as a means for the development of semi-arid regions and also to help the poor households with little or no land to find a viable source of livelihood. However, their potential is yet to be realised thanks to various problems pointed out above including the neglect of CPRs and general indifference to this sector inspite of the increasing demand for meat and milk.

REFERENCES

Acharya, R.M. (1984), "Research and Development in Sheep and Goat", Indian Farming, Vol. XXXIV, No. 1, April.

Ahuja, Kanta and M.S. Rathore (1987), Goats and Goat Keepers : A Socio-Economic Study, Printwell Pub., Jaipur.

Alaev, L.B. (1984), "South India—The System of Agriculture Production", in I.Habib and T. Ray Chaudhary (ed) Cambridge Economic History of India, Vol. I, Orient Longman.

Amir, P. (1988), "Economics of Goat Meat Production", in Devendra, C. (ed), Goat Meat Production in Asia, Proceedings of a Workshop held in Tando Jam, Pakistan, 13-18 March 1988, International Development Research Centre, Canada.

Askew and Mitchell (1978), as quoted by Soedomo R. *et al.* "Non-Leguminous Trees and Shrubs as Forage for Ruminants", in G.J. Blair *et. al.*, Forage in South-East Asian and South Pacific Agriculture, ACIAR, 1986.

Bardhan, Pranab (1982), "Agrarian class Formation in India", Journal of Peasant Studies, Vol. 10 (1), October.

Batie, Sandra S. (1982), "Sustainable Development : Challenges to the Profession of Agricultural Economics", American Journal of Agricultural Economics, Vol 71, No. 5, December.

Bhasin, N.R. (1988), "Marketing of Goat Meat", in Devendra, C. Goat Meat Production in Asia, Proceedings of a Workshop held in Tando Jam, Pakistan, 13-18 March, IDRC, 268 e, Canada.

Borkar V.V. and Nadkarni M.V. (1975), Impact of Drought on Rural Life, Popular Prakashan, Bombay.

CAZRI (Central Arid Zone Research Institute) (1983), "Outlines of the Technologies for Reconstruction of the Arid Zone", Technical Bulletin No. 7, CAZRI, Jodhpur, India.

Census of India, 1981, Series-9, Karnataka, Part II-B (1) : Primary Census Abstract, General Population, 1984.

Census of India, 1981, Series-9 Karnataka, Paper 4 of 1984, Occupied Residential Houses and Households.

Census of India, 1981, Series-9 Karnataka, District Census Hand Book, Kolar District, Part XIII-A&B Village and Town Directory.

Chauhan S.K. and T.V. Moorti (1990), Economics of Sheep Farming, Mittal Publications, New Delhi.

CLRI (Central Leather Research Institute) (1974), Monthly Statistics of Foregin Trade of India, Vol. I, Exports and Re-Exports, Directorate General of Commercial Intelligence and Statistics, Calcutta, India.

Deoghare P.R. *et al.* (1990), "Goat Rearing in Rural Economy", paper presented at the National Seminar on Economics of Agriculture with reference to viability and sustainability of marginal and small farmers, organised by National Institute of Rural Development, Hyderabad, India, during October.

Devendra, C. (1987), "Small Ruminant Production System", in Devendra, C (ed). Small Ruminant Production Systems in South and Southeast Asia, Proceedings of a Workshop held in Begor, Indonesia, 6-10, October, 1986, International Development Research Centre, Canada.

Devendra, C. and G.B. Mcleroy (1982), Goat and Sheep Production in the Topics, Longman, London.

Damodaran, A. (1987), "Structural Dimensions of Fodder Crisis—A Village Study in Karnataka", Economic and Political Weekly, Vol. XXII, No. 13, Review of Agriculture, March 28.

F.A.O. (Food and Agricultural Organisation of the United Nations) (1998), Year Book Production, 1997, Vol. 51, F.A.O., Rome.

Gadgil, Madhav and Madhulika Sinha (1986), "The Biomass Budget of Karnataka", in Cecil J Saldanha, Karnataka-State of Environment Report---1984-85, Centre for Taxonomic Studies, Bangalore.

Gopalakrishnan C.A. and G.M.M. Lal (1985), Livestock and Poultry Enterprises for Rural Development, Vikas Publishing House, New Delhi.

Gutierrez-Aleman, Nestor (1983), Sheep and Goat Production Systems in the Sertao Region of Northeast Brazil : A Characterization and Linear Programming Analysis, Ph.D. thesis, Purdue University, University Microfilms International, Ann Arbor.

Hardin, Garrett (1968), "The Tragedy of Commons", Science, 162 : 1243-1248.

Harriss, John (1982), Capitalism and Peasant Farming : Agrarian Structure and Ideology in Northern Tamil Nadu, Oxford University Press, Delhi.

Hart, R.D. and H.C. Knipscheer (1987), "Characteristics and Socio-Economic Aspects of Small Ruminant Production Systems : An Analytical Framework", in Devendra, C. (ed). Small Ruminant Production Systems in South and Southeast Asia, Proceedings of a Workshop held in Begor, Indonesia, 6-10, October, 1986, International Development Research Centre, Canada.

India, Government of, Agricultural Situation in India, October, 1983 to November, 1986, Directorate of Economics and Statistics, Ministry of Agriculture, New Delhi.

India, Government of (1987), Report of the Task Force to Evaluate the Impact of Sheep and Goat Rearing in Ecologically Fragile Zone, Ministry of Agriculture, Department of Agriculture and Co-operation, New Delhi.

India, Government of, National Accounts Statistics, 1983 and 1989, Central Statistical Organisation, Ministry of Planning.

India, Government of, Estimates of State Domestic Product, 1985, 1987, 1989, Central Statistical Organisation, Ministry of Planning.

India, Government of, Indian Livestock Census, Vol. II, 1956, 1966,

1972, 1987 and 1992, Directorate of Economics and Statistics, New Delhi.

India, Government of, Indian Livestock Census (1987), Ministry of Agriculture, Department of Animal Husbandry and Dairying, New Delhi, 1995.

India, Government of, Indian Agriculture in Brief, 7th, 17th, 19th, 20th, 21st and 22nd editions, Directorate of Economics and Statistics, Department of Agriculture and Co-operation, New Delhi.

India, Government of, Indian Agricultural Statistics, Vol. II, 1974-75 to 1976-77, Directorate of Economics and Statistics, Ministry of Agriculture, New Delhi.

Ivory, D.A. and Armiadi Semali (1987), "Production Systems Based on Annual Cropping", in Devendra C. (ed) Small Ruminant Production Systems in South and Southeast Asia, Proceedings of Workshop held in Bogor, Indonesia, 6-10, October, 1986, International Development Research Centre, Canada.

Jodha, N.S. (1986), "Common Porperty Resources and Rural Poor in Dry Regions of India", Economic and Political Weekly, Vol. 21 (27).

Jodha, N.S. (1966), "A Semi-Nomadic Farm Family (From the Arid Zone of Rajasthan)", A/D/C paper, December, The Agricultural Development Council, Inc. New York.

Kalia, H.R. and A.R. Rajapurohit (1989), "Goat Rearing in India : Techno-Economics, Managerial and Policy Issues", in Indian Society of Agricultural Economics, Livestock Economy of India, Oxford & IBH, New Delhi.

Kalia, H.R. (1985), "Goat Vis-a-Vis 'Garibi", Agricultural Situation in India, Vol. XL, No. 5, August.

Karnataka, Government of (1985), 13th Livestock Census, 1983, Department of Animal Husbandry and Veterinary Services, Bangalore.

Karnataka, Government of, Report on Sample Survey for Estimation of Production of Milk, Egg, Wool and Meat from 1976-77 to 1984-85, Directorate of Animal Husbandry and Veterinary Services, Bangalore.

Karnataka, Government of, Official Records of the Department of Animal Husbandry and Veterinary Services, 1987-88, Bangalore.

Karnataka, Government of, Official Records (1989-90), Directorate of Economics and Statistics, Bangalore.

Karnataka, Government of, 14th Quinquennial Livestock Census 1990, Department of Animal Husbandry and Veterinary Services, Bangalore.

Karnataka, Government of, Statistical Abstract of Karnataka, 1978-79, Bureau of Economics and Statistics, Bangalore.

Karnataka, Government of, State Domestic Product—Karnataka, 1980-81 and 1990-91 to 1997-98, Department of Economics and Statistics, Bangalore.

Karnataka, Government of, Report on Integrated Sample Survey for Estimation of Production of Milk, Egg. Wool and Meat for the Year 1995-96, Directorated of Animal Husbandry and Veterinary Services in Karnataka, Bangalore.

Lal, G.M.M. (1982), Commercial Banks and Goat Development Programmes, Himalaya Publishing House, Bombay.

Mace, Ruth (1989), "Gambling with Goats : Variability in Herd Growth Among Restocked Pastoralists in Kenya", Pastoral Development Network, Paper, 24a, Overseas Development Institute, London.

McCorkle, Constance M. et al. (1987), "Highlights from Sociological (CRSP) Research on Small Ruminants", Pastoral Development Network, Pape 24d, Overseas Development Institute, London.

Moore, M.P. (1978), "Some Micro-Economic Aspects of the Livestock Economy", Indian Journal of Agricultural Economics, XXXIII, Jan-March.

Mukundan G. and S. Balakrishnan (1987), "Integration of Small Ruminants and Tree Cropping in South Indian", in Devendra C. (ed) Small Ruminant Production Systems in South and Southeast Asia, Proceedings of a Workshop held in Bogor, Indonesia, 6-10, October, 1986, International Development Research Centre, Canada.

Mysore, Government of, Annual Season and Crop Report, 1956-57, 1960-61 and 1966-67, The Department of Statistics, Bangalore.

NABARD (National Bank for Agriculture and Rural Development) (1982), Sheep Rearing in Nalgonda District of Andhra Pradesh (An Ex-Post Evaluation Study), NABARD.

Nadkarni M.V. (1985), Socio-Economic Conditions of Droughtprone Areas, Concept Publishing Company, New Delhi.

NCA (National Commission on Agriculture) (1976), Report of the National Commision on Agriculture, Part VII, Animal Husbandry, NCA, Ministry of Agriculture, Government of India, New Delhi.

National Accounts Statistics of India—1950-51 to 1996-97, Economic and Political Weekly Research Foundation, Mumbai, October, 1998.

Pandeya, S.C. (1988), Status of Indian Rangelands, Presidential Address, 3rd International Range Land Congress, November, Jodhpur, India.

Ram, K. Anantha and K.K. Vyas, Economics of Rearing Sheep in Arid Rajasthan, AES-Res. Report No. 1, Division of Agricultural Economics and Statistics, Central Arid Zone Research Institute, Jodhpur, India.

Ranjhan, S.K. (1986), "Sources of Feed for Ruminants Production in South-East Asia", in Blair G.J. *et al.* (eds) Forages in South-East Asian and South Pacific Agriculture, (Proceedings of an International Workshop held at Cisarus, Indonesia, August, 1985), ACIAR.

Rao, K. Seshagiri (1988), "By-Products from Gaot Meat Production and their Marketing in India", in Devendra, Ç. Goat Meat Production in Asia, Proceedings of a Workshop held in Tando Jam, Pakistan, 13-18 March, IDRC, 268 e, Canada.

Rath, Nilakantha (1992), "Economics of Sheep and Goats in Maharashtra", Indian Journal of Agriculture Economics, Vol. XLVII, No. 1, January-March 1992.

Rice, B. Lewis (1897), Mysore, A Gazetteer Compiled for Government, Vol. I, Mysore in General, Westminister, Archibald Constable and Company, 2 Whitehall Garden, S.W. MDCCCXVII.

Shankarnarayan, K.A., Bohra, H.C. and P.K. Ghosh (1985), "The Goat-An Appropriate Animal for Arid and Semi-Arid Regions", Economic and Political Weekly, Vol. XX, Nos. 45, 46 and 47, special number, November.

Singh, S.P. *et al.* (1990), "Estimation of Meat Production in States and Union Territories of India", Agricultural Situation in India, February.

Singh, Ranveer and R. Swarup (1985), Economics of Sheep Rearing in Himachal Pradesh, Agro-Economic Research Centre, Himachal Pradesh University, Shimla.

Sinha, P. and A.K. Giri (1989), "Consumption of Livestock Products—Analysis and Comparison of Data of NSS 32nd and 38th Rounds", in Livestock Economy of India, Indian Society of Agricultural Economics, Oxford and IBH, New Delhi.

Sundaram, P. *et al.* (1981), An Economic Analysis of Sheep Rearing as a Farm Enterprise, A.H. Econ. Research Report No. 5, Department of Animal Husbandry Economics, Madras Veterinary College, Madras, India.

Swain, N. *et al.* (1986), "Relative Performance and Economics of Sheep and Goats under Production Remuneration Management System", Indian Journal of Animal Sciences, 56(5), May.

Van Eys J.E. *et al.* (1987), "Feed Resources and Feeding Systems for

Small Ruminants in South and Southeast Asia", in Devendra C. (ed) Small Ruminant Production Systems in South and Southeast Asia, Proceedings of a Workshop held in Bogor, Indonesia, 6-10, October, 1986, International Development Research Centre, Canada.

Winrock International (1983), Sheep and Goats in Developing Countries—their present and potential Role, the World Bank, Washington, DC, U.S.A.

World Bank (1991), Environmental Assessment Sourcebook, Vol. II, Sectoral Guidelines, World Bank Technical Paper Number 140, Environment Department, The World Bank, Washington, D.C., pp. 103-112.

Index